SOUTHERN LITERARY STUDIES

Fred Hobson, Editor

POEMS OF PURE IMAGINATION

POEMS OF
PURE IMAGINATION

*Robert Penn Warren and
the Romantic Tradition*

Lesa Carnes Corrigan

Louisiana State University Press   *Baton Rouge*

Copyright © 1999 Louisiana State University Press
All rights reserved
Manufactured in the United States of America
First printing

08 07 06 05 04 03 02 01 00 99
5 4 3 2 1

Designer: Melanie Samaha
Typeface: Adobe Caslon
Typesetter: Coghill Composition
Printer and binder: Edwards Brothers, Inc.

Library of Congress Cataloging-in-Publication Data

Corrigan, Lesa Carnes, 1967–
    Poems of pure imagination : Robert Penn Warren and the Romantic
tradition / Lesa Carnes Corrigan.
        p.   cm. — (Southern literary studies)
    Includes bibliographical references and index.
    ISBN 0-8071-2408-7 (cl. : alk. paper)
    1. Warren, Robert Penn, 1905–   —Criticism and interpretation.
    2. Warren, Robert Penn, 1905–   —Knowledge—Literature.
    3. American poetry—English influences.   4. Southern States—In
literature.   5. Romanticism—Southern States.   6. Imagination.
    I. Title.   II. Series.
    PS3545.A748Z657   1999
    813'.52—dc21   99-32047
                                                                        CIP

The portions of Robert Penn Warren's works quoted herein are copyright © 1923, 1953,
1955, 1958, 1975, 1979, 1985 by Robert Penn Warren. Reprinted by permission of William Morris Agency, Inc., on behalf of the Author.

To my parents,
Tom and Gail Carnes—for everything

Contents

Acknowledgments

The basic premise of this study is not altogether original, but I hope that my careful scrutiny and detailed reading of Warren's poetry result in a solid and helpful piece of scholarship, something that both lovers of as well as newcomers to Warren's poetry can find useful and enjoyable. In addition to the scholars whose works are noted in the text (and without whose pioneering studies this work would not have been possible), I am grateful to many colleagues and friends who have encouraged me through the years. I would especially like to thank Hugh Ruppersburg at the University of Georgia for his patience, guidance, wisdom, and general good humor. Under his tutelage and careful eye, my study blossomed into the work we have here. I gratefully acknowledge the assistance of Anne Williams, Douglas Anderson, Hubert McAlexander, and Blue Calhoun at the University of Georgia, all of whom continue to support my scholarly work. Of course, many dear friends and relatives gave me the love and encouragement I needed during the long days and nights of vision and revision: Diana Barrett; Dennis Michael and Phyllis Corrigan; Darren and Cris Felty; Gayle Hannah; Charley Henley; Emily Hipchen; Maura Mandyck; Kenneth Millard; Eileen and Chris Perillo; and Lynn, Jeff, Christopher, and Brandon Thrash. To my colleagues at the University of Alabama I owe special thanks, particularly to Robert Halli and William Ulmer, who prompted my efforts and applauded my successes every step of the way. I would also like to thank John Easterly at Louisiana State University Press. Our mutual love of baseball as well as his generosity and helpfulness created a most felicitous editor/author relationship. And to Dennis Corrigan I extend my heartfelt and sincere gratitude for all his patience and care.

Abbreviations

Published by Random House and its affiliates:

BD	*Brother to Dragons* [1979]
BD [1953]	*Brother to Dragons*
NSE	*New and Selected Essays*
NR	*Night Rider*
PCT	*A Place to Come To*
SE	*Selected Essays*
WET	*World Enough and Time*

From other publishers:

AKM	*All the King's Men*
CP	*Collected Poems*
DP	*Democracy and Poetry*
"Knowledge"	"Knowledge and the Image of Man"
PF	*Portrait of a Father*

POEMS OF PURE IMAGINATION

Introduction

Ever the astute observer, especially of his friends and poetic counterparts, Allen Tate saw early in Robert Penn Warren the first glimpses of the Romantic vision that would become the hallmark of Warren's most powerful and mature work. In the same year that Tate described the gangly, red-haired youth from Guthrie, Kentucky, as "a wonder," he composed these lines in wry but admiring tribute to Warren:

> You hold your eager head
> Too high in the air, you walk
> As if the sleepy dead
> Had never fallen to drowse
> From the sublimest talk
> Of many a vehement house.

Tate's 1924 poem, entitled "To a Romantic," may have been in part poking fun at the young man's tentative idealism, yet it recognizes in Warren a powerful yearning to explore the truths that allow one to live meaningfully.[1] Warren's search for "Truth" inspired some of the

---

1. Allen Tate, *Collected Poems, 1919–1976* (New York: Farrar, Straus Giroux, 1977), 7.

finest poetry and fiction produced in this century by an American writer, and his amazing diversity and scope reveal the range of influences that went into the shaping of America's first poet laureate. This book focuses on one specific influence, a group of poets who lived and wrote a little more than a century before Warren published his first poems in the *Fugitive* at Vanderbilt University. His study of the English Romantics in the 1940s led to a form of "conversion" experience, out of which emerged the sense of purpose and vision that dominates his work until the end of his writing career. On an aesthetic and philosophical level, Warren found the concepts espoused by the English Romantics similar to his own ideas about the human need for truth, the necessity of knowledge (despite the costs), and as he states in his essay "Knowledge and the Image of Man," man's "continual and intimate interpenetration" (186) with the world.

To call Warren a Romantic demands an acceptance, as Joseph Blotner claims in "Romantic Elements in Faulkner," that "Romanticism is not a literary movement circumscribed in time like a political administration but rather a constellation of intellectual and emotional attitudes and certain embodiments of them given expression in literature." Warren's Romanticism does not preclude the evidence of other philosophical considerations in his writing, yet the numerous critics who have pointed out the increasingly Romantic thrust of Warren's writings over the span of his career lend credence to the argument that his development as a writer took inspiration and direction from his reading of the English Romantics. Victor Strandberg asserts that Warren's "essentially Romantic sensibility" offers a "redeeming, self-transcending vision," providing a fusion between self and nature. James Justus's claim that Warren is "a latter-day Romantic" arises from his evaluation of Warren as a writer who, like his Romantic predecessors, insisted upon the "unified indivisibility of moral action" and demanded that it be judged "in terms of its own entirety, as a total process."[2] Even critics who have focused on the elements of nat-

2. Joseph Blotner, "Romantic Elements in Faulkner," in *Romantic and Modern: Revaluations of Literary Tradition*, ed. George Bornstein (Pittsburgh: University of Pittsburgh Press, 1977), 208; Victor Strandberg, *The*

uralism in Warren's works allow that he does not rest easily with determinism or the notion of an external world devoid of meaning.

Warren's progress toward his Romantic vision, however, is gradual and often tempered by the skepticism so evident in twentieth-century thought. His early poetry, highly imitative of Eliot and Pound and the Metaphysical poets of the seventeenth century, exhibits the careful attention to craft that John Crowe Ransom had encouraged among his students but little of the exuberance that characterizes Warren's later poems. As Patricia Wallace points out, "an embrace of the world was not readily available to Warren in his early models," yet from the beginning we hear the urgent questioning that energizes the later poetry. Warren's Romanticism, like that of the Romantic poets themselves, was not a single, homogeneous manifestation that appeared suddenly at the beginning of his career and remained constant until the end. There are certain continuities in theme throughout Warren's work—the search for identity, the "thirst to know the power and nature of Time" (*CP*, 379) (from the Augustinian epigraph to *Being Here*), and the need to comprehend the significance of memory and the past—but Warren's approach to these concerns develops and changes throughout his long career, exhibiting the capacity of renewal that Charles Olson calls "the will to change."[3]

Like William Butler Yeats, another twentieth-century Romantic, Warren adapted the Romantic metaphors of the imagination to a modern context, making the poet's quest for images the paradigmatic act of mind. In true Romantic fashion, both writers exploit memory in striking juxtapositions of past and present. In this way, the world of memory is transformed into imagined realms where the interplay of innocence and maturity points toward the relationship between self and other, that other being not only the natural world that exists

Poetic Vision of Robert Penn Warren (Lexington: University Press of Kentucky, 1977), 190; James Justus, *The Achievement of Robert Penn Warren* (Baton Rouge: Louisiana State University Press, 1981), 113.

3. Patricia Wallace, "Warren, with Ransom and Tate," in *Columbia History of American Poetry*, ed. Jay Parini (New York: Columbia University Press, 1993), 492, 493; Charles Olson, quoted *ibid.*, 493.

within time but also the interior world of memory that exists outside of time. In his conception of Romanticism, Warren is Yeats's American counterpart, and several critics (including a "belated convert" to Warren's poetry, Harold Bloom) have compared the ways in which the two poets apply Romantic concepts to a distinctly modern consciousness. Cleanth Brooks, Warren's longtime friend and collaborator, asserts in *The Hidden God* that, like Yeats, Warren exhibits "a tough-minded insistence upon the facts, including the realistic and ugly facts—a fierce refusal to shield one's eyes from what is there." As careful readers may notice, Warren consistently reveals the dangers inherent in overt idealism. Any transcendence or "redemption" in his fictive or poetic world appears, at best, illusory. Yet, as Warren writes in his 1951 essay on Conrad's *Nostromo*, "The last wisdom is for man to realize that though his values are illusions, the illusion is necessary, is infinitely precious, is the mark of his human achievement, and is, in the end, his only truth" (*NSE*, 149). Like Shelley's "painted veil which those who live / Call Life," Warren's vision of the world paradoxically encourages truth seeking but at the same time cautions that the search itself may be more important than the Truth (which is not likely to be found) and may provide the clearest sense of one's place in nature, society, and history.[4]

At the heart of much of Warren's work, as John Burt, William Bedford Clark, and Hugh Ruppersburg assert, lies a preoccupation with America's past, present, and future. Emerging from and contributing to his vision of America is an ethos appropriated from the English Romantics, diluted only by the divergent strains of American Romanticism and adapted to a distinctly American terrain. Warren was a Romantic visionary, but his Romanticism (and I capitalize "Romanticism" to avoid confusion with its use in reference to general idealism) achieves dimensions beyond merely the transposition of concepts assigned to the English Romantic poets. The Romantic vi-

---

4. Cleanth Brooks, *The Hidden God: Studies in Hemingway, Faulkner, Yeats, Eliot, and Warren* (New Haven: Yale University Press, 1963), 98; Percy Bysshe Shelley, *Shelley's Poetry and Prose*, ed. Donald H. Reiman and Sharon B. Powers (New York: Norton, 1977), 312.

sion that Warren incorporates into much of his work combines the tempered aesthetics of Wordsworth with Yeats's awareness of historical violence and modern estrangement. In Warren's fiction and poetry, we find figures resembling Coleridge's Mariner lamenting crimes against the American landscape. Warren's recurrent concern over the fate of poetry and the arts in general has as its antecedent Shelley's "Defence of Poetry," and like Keats's nightingale, Warren's "sunset hawk" becomes the symbolic equivalent of the poetic imagination and the human desire for merger with nature. These comparisons should not suggest a sort of "grab-bag" mentality on Warren's part, nor am I proposing that he applied certain Romantic themes and images in a loose or random fashion. These links do, however, exhibit how closely Warren associated his most deeply felt intuitions about art and life with the overarching philosophies of the Romantics. Late in his life, Warren told Bill Moyers, "I yearn for significance, for life as significance."[5] This yearning, which for Warren provided a stay against naturalistic despair, aligns him with the Romantics in their insistence upon the possibilities of joy in a ruined and lost world, transitory and fleeting glimpses of transcendence that are nonetheless rooted in experience and the external world. For Warren as well as for the Romantics, poetic vision is always earned, but it is never finite.

It is not surprising that Warren felt drawn to the philosophical and poetic positions of the English Romantics. Born and raised in rural Kentucky, he developed a deep-rooted sense of respect for his native region and its history and folklore. His father was a highly learned and literate man who wrote poetry and knew Greek and Latin. Warren's grandfather, a Confederate veteran, quoted Byron while recounting the campaigns of Nathan Bedford Forrest.[6] Warren

5. Robert Penn Warren, "A Conversation with Robert Penn Warren," interview by Bill Moyers, in *Talking with Robert Penn Warren*, ed. Floyd C. Watkins, John T. Hiers, and Mary Louise Weaks (Athens: University of Georgia Press, 1990), 214.

6. In a 1953 "self-interview" that appeared in the *New York Herald Tribune Book Review* shortly after the publication of *Brother to Dragons*, Warren

remembers his grandfather being "soaked in poetry," primarily the English Romantics, and one of Warren's favorite poems as a child was Coleridge's *Rime of the Ancient Mariner* (*PF*, 37). The eclecticism of Warren's upbringing fostered in him a love for language and history as well as for the workings of the natural world. As a young boy he wanted to be a painter, a sort of "boy naturalist" much like the figure of Audubon, who inspired Warren's 1969 poem. As a teenager, imbued with a deep sense of history and the romance of the past, Warren dreamed of becoming a naval officer ("I was determined to be an admiral for the Pacific fleet," he told William Ferris in 1979), but an accident that caused him to lose sight in one eye cost him an appointment to Annapolis.[7] He went instead to Vanderbilt University, intending to become a chemical engineer. After only three weeks of uninspiring chemistry courses, Warren turned his attention toward his literature class, where his potential as a writer captured the attention of his freshman English professor, John Crowe Ransom, as well as his classmates such as Allen Tate and Donald Davidson.

Following the devastation and trauma of the First World War, Warren's early years at Vanderbilt coincided with one of the most tumultuous periods in American history. Writers and thinkers critical of Western culture challenged prevailing artistic forms and cultural standards, and Vanderbilt University, referred to as the center of Modernism in the South by William Jennings Bryan (although not in the most complimentary light), felt the surge of dramatic innovations. Times of social tension often produce aesthetic and philosophical tensions as well, resulting in an outpouring of literature exploring the need for a new sense of self rooted in the motives, emotions, and imaginations of the people. M. H. Abrams maintains that the "need to justify the existence of poets and the reading of poetry becomes

---

spoke of his grandfather as a "'visionary' . . . looming much larger than life, the living symbol of the wild action and romance of the past." See Robert Penn Warren, "A Self-Interview," in *Talking with Robert Penn Warren*, ed. Watkins et al., 2.

7. William Ferris, "Robert Penn Warren: 'My Cup Ran Over,'" *Reckon: The Magazine of Southern Culture* 1 (Premiere issue 1995): 125.

acute in times of social strain." Throughout history, the greatest literature has often been written in the wake of revolutions and wars, and the cultural and political atmosphere that marked the beginning of the Romantic era in Great Britain strikingly resembles the post–World War I period in America. Abrams observes the similarities between the Romantic period in the nineteenth century and the decades of the 1920s and 1930s in America: "The English Romantic era, which occurred hard upon the French Revolution, amid war and the rumors of war, and in the stress of social and political adjustments to the Industrial Revolution, was comparable to our own period between the two World Wars."[8] For the first generation of Romantics in England—Blake, Wordsworth, and Coleridge—the French Revolution represented a cultural, intellectual, and moral as well as political crisis. The aftermath of the Revolution shattered the apocalyptic and millennial transformations anticipated by the early Romantics, and they were faced instead with the prospect of widespread industrialization and the diminishment of a largely rural and agrarian way of life.

Similarly, the aftermath of World War I affected national as well as international consciousness, and Warren and his fellow southerners at Vanderbilt discerned that the South was by no means immune to this period of radical readjustment. Rather, the South's position as a relatively isolated and closed society made it especially vulnerable in the face of modern change. In a 1967 conversation with Roy Newquist, Warren offered his hypothesis of the South's literary flowering after World War I: "I think it happened this way: The world of the South was frozen from 1865 to 1917, when the First World War came along. Things happened there, but the pattern of thought wasn't disturbed. There were no new ideas, no basic changes in society. The First World War shattered the frozen quality of the South." Warren comments that his generation "benefited" from the shock of this period, but it was "the generation of John Crowe Ransom, Allen Tate,

---

8. M. H. Abrams, *The Mirror and the Lamp: Romantic Theory and the Critical Tradition* (New York: Norton, 1971), 326.

and William Faulkner [who] made the real crossover."[9] As two of the central figures of the Fugitive group at Vanderbilt, Ransom and Tate themselves wrote and encouraged the sixteen-year-old Warren to write the type of poetry that did not sentimentalize or idealize the South but instead offered a commentary on the plight of the modern individual. The Fugitives were southerners, to be sure, but ambivalently and often self-consciously southern, attempting to cut through and distance themselves from the "veil of myth" that surrounded so much about the South.

Although the Fugitives adamantly shunned what might be called the "Father Ryan" school of poetry, they were very much aware of the South's uniqueness as a region rich in history and folklore yet trapped in a form of cultural myopia. The Fugitives and other southern writers of Warren's generation had a distinctly European orientation, with the modernism of Pound and Eliot serving as the model for much for their poetry. Although Yeats was not a modernist in the same vein as Pound and Eliot, he also served as an important figure for the Fugitives, chiefly because his poetry embodied a similar fusion of regional identity with universal concerns. Warren commented to Marshall Walker in 1969 that the poetry written by the Fugitives shared a special affinity with the work of Yeats and other Irish writers: "It was part of a turning back, a turning from their [the Fugitives'] interest in poetry to try to see the setting of the kind of poetry that interested them. The notion of Ireland was deep in this . . . the notion of a somewhat backward society in an outlying place with a different tradition and a rich folk-life, facing the big modern machine. This notion was in the background, talked about not as a model but as a parallel somehow." Although the South lacked much of Ireland's religious and racial cohesion, the two cultures shared similar historical situations of conflict and defeat, and as Warren told David Farrell, both were viewed as "primitive [and] retarded people

---

9. Eleanor Clark and Robert Penn Warren, "Conversation: Eleanor Clark and Robert Penn Warren," interview by Roy Newquist, in *Talking with Robert Penn Warren*, ed. Watkins et al., 87.

against the great, powerful industrial organization."[10] Like Yeats, the Fugitives did not avert their eyes from the problems of their native soil, nor did they advocate an ahistorical "New South" that attempted to eradicate the past in a wave of technological advances and industry.

The Fugitive poets were strictly a literary circle, not to be confused with the Agrarians, another group that had its start at Vanderbilt and involved many of the members of the Fugitive group. In the South in particular, a region only a few decades removed from civil strife and defeat, the threat of economic and industrial domination challenged the Fugitives and subsequently the Agrarians to formulate intellectual, social, and literary theories in reaction to an increasing sense of alienation from their society. Although technically the Fugitives and the Agrarians were two separate and distinct schools—one primarily literary and the other political—they overlapped in certain areas. Like the English Romantics a century earlier, both groups saw potentially dangerous transformations occurring in the society around them, especially in the public's increasing apathy (and at times hostility) toward the arts.

Yet despite several generic shared concerns, the Fugitives and the Agrarians had very different agendas. The Fugitives did not initially set out to propose particular doctrines about poetry; rather, they banded together because of their love for poetry—they called themselves "amateurs" in the literal sense of the word, lovers of poetry as well as of good conversation and good food. They did not consciously construct their group as a "movement" (as with the contemporaneous Imagists), yet the members of the Fugitive group were able critics of what they observed about society and art.[11] The Fugitives shunned

10. Robert Penn Warren, "Robert Penn Warren: An Interview," by Marshall Walker, *ibid.*, 150; and "Reminiscences: A Conversation with Robert Penn Warren," by David Farrell, *ibid.*, 291.

11. In *The Fugitive Poets: Modern Southern Poetry in Perspective* (Nashville: J. S. Saunders, 1991), William Pratt notes that "what began as simply an informal fraternity, or philosophers' club, developed by gradual stages into a serious literary school with its own journal, and an audience that reached beyond the city into the region, the nation, and the world" (xvii).

any singular association with antebellum modes of thought, and as Ransom wrote in the preface to the first issue of the group's literary magazine, "*The Fugitive* flees from nothing faster than from the high-caste Brahmins of the Old South."[12] In contrast, the Agrarians were deliberately and often aggressively prosouthern, to some extent nostalgically promoting the belief that the rural, farm-based life was an ideal to be sought and regained. As John L. Stewart points out in *The Burden of Time,* his study of the Fugitive poets, at the core of Warren's basic philosophy was an essentially Agrarian sensibility, and much of his work reflects the dominant ideas, themes, and attitudes of the Agrarian movement. But by the time Warren returned to Vanderbilt in the 1930s and joined the Agrarians, he had already begun to explore many of the principal themes in his early poems as well as in novels such as *Night Rider* and *At Heaven's Gate*—the inchoate longing for lost innocence, the struggle for self-knowledge, and the meaning of history.

Warren's Fugitive years marked only the beginning of his long career, but many of the ideas he conceived during his time with the group in Nashville endured throughout his sixty-five years as a writer.[13] While the Fugitives were not active revolutionaries in the same sense that some of the English Romantic poets were (Byron and Shelley in particular), their proposals and beliefs about poetry corresponded to the consensual philosophies held by most of the English Romantics. Both groups maintained that the visionary qualities of the poet made him different from other men because of his "in-

12. Ransom quoted in John L. Stewart, *The Burden of Time: The Fugitives and Agrarians* (Princeton: Princeton University Press, 1965), 25.

13. See William Bedford Clark, "Young Warren and the Problematics of Faith," *Mississippi Quarterly* 45, no. 1 (winter 1991–92): 29–39. As Clark acknowledges, "Warren's Fugitive poems, creditable enough in the company they keep, give slight indication of the stature he would come to enjoy in the second half of the century." Clark also advises, however, that we not discount Warren's earliest poetry as mere juvenilia because "we stand to learn much about the formative imagination that gradually gave voice to some of the most striking poetry of our time."

tense sensibility"; a poet, Wordsworth said, "differs from other men because he is 'endowed with more lively sensibility, more enthusiasm and tenderness.'"[14] Coleridge and Shelley also spoke of the "susceptibility to passion" that the poet experienced because of this intense sensibility. Although Blake (one of Warren's favorite poets, as he acknowledged in an interview with Ralph Ellison) preceded Wordsworth, Coleridge, and the other Romantics and never identified with them, he too attested to the belief in the poet's visionary endowments, and his elevation of the poetic imagination to the level of the divine places him within the conceptual ideology of the other Romantics.

Warren's firm belief in the intrinsic value of poetry made him a candidate for an integral role in the American New Critical movement, and by the early 1940s, Warren, along with fellow Fugitives John Crowe Ransom and Allen Tate, had contributed to the establishment of New Criticism within the academy. In *The Cultural Politics of the New Criticism*, Mark Jancovich notes that while Warren, Ransom, and Tate remained friends, their initial agreement on literary and social criticism began to diverge almost at the same time that they aided in heralding the widespread acceptance of the New Criticism. Yet these three integral figures of that movement retained their initial conviction that the poet was somehow endowed with special powers, an attribute that Art Berman calls "a reversion to Coleridge." Berman goes further to contend that "the New Criticism could not help but be influenced by Romanticism," particularly in light of Coleridge's theory of the "reconciliation of opposites," an idea that exemplifies New Criticism's focus on the "formation of complex ideas through combination."[15]

Warren's role in the New Critical movement has perhaps garnered him more scorn than praise, especially in recent years, mainly because

14. Wordsworth quoted in Abrams, *Mirror and the Lamp*, 102.

15. Mark Jancovich, *The Cultural Politics of the New Criticism* (Cambridge: Cambridge University Press, 1993), 103; Art Berman, *From the New Criticism to Deconstruction: The Reception of Structuralism and Poststructuralism* (Urbana: University of Illinois Press, 1988), 46, 48.

he has been unfairly lumped with other New Critics who are currently considered ultra-conservative, narrow, "undoubtedly reactionary," and "perhaps bigoted." Many literary scholars who know of Warren primarily through his New Critical essay on Coleridge may perceive him as an inseparable third member of what Hyatt Waggoner humorously calls "the Ransom–Tate–Warren trio."[16] One of the chief attacks on the New Criticism suggests that it ignores the social and historical environment of the text under examination. Other detractors charge that the New Criticism, due to the cultural milieu of its creators, smacks of a certain antiquated paternalism. Jancovich's study of the "cultural politics" of the New Critics vigorously defends Warren in particular against the claims of elitism and historical negation, even at times championing Warren's critical and literary endeavors over his longtime counterparts Ransom and Tate. Warren never abandoned some of the most basic ideas he shared with other Fugitives and New Critics, especially his suspicions that the "kind of knowledge that . . . the Romantic poets . . . speak of" cannot survive in our increasingly abstract and technological world (*DP*, 48). This knowledge, the power of imagination and the intuitive comprehension of "passion," would become obsolete as the individual divorced himself from one of the most vital means of exploring "the deep, dark inwardness of his nature and his fate" (*DP*, 31), a faculty Warren assigns to poetry. Warren's ideas about poetry (and literature in general) offer a reconciliation of the personal with the universal, the subjective with the objective. Out of his New Critical explorations emerged Warren's personal aesthetic that poetry, while possessing inherent meaning in and of itself, must also encourage the individual to seek active engagement with the world.

In his work with Ransom and, later, with Cleanth Brooks, Warren developed his own critical language rooted in a form of resurgent humanism, and his criticism of the 1940s exhibits fundamentally Romantic responses and attitudes. Warren's early conviction that poetry

---

16. Berman, *From the New Criticism to Deconstruction*, 86; Hyatt Waggoner, *American Poets: From the Puritans to the Present* (Baton Rouge: Louisiana State University Press, 1968), 547.

provides ontological knowledge, an idea nourished by his work with the Fugitives, the Agrarians, and the New Critics, became the central defining notion of his criticism as well as of his poetry and fiction. From the mid-1940s until the early 1950s, Warren produced some of his finest criticism and fiction (including the Pulitzer Prize-winning *All the King's Men* and *World Enough and Time*), but during this period he encountered one of the most serious challenges of his poetic career. Personal and aesthetic crises affected him both psychologically and artistically, and the ensuing "drought" plagued him for most of the 1940s. "I must have started fifty short poems," he told Richard B. Sale in 1969. "Not a one panned out. I threw them all away, and some of them were going okay. I couldn't finish them; they died on me. For ten years, every one of them died."[17]

Unable to finish a short poem, Warren began an intense process of self-evaluation and exploration of other genres. Literary criticism became one of his central preoccupations, and his involvement in the New Critical movement established him as an important voice among literary theorists, especially with the publication of his essay on Coleridge's *Rime of the Ancient Mariner*. Aside from its critical significance, "A Poem of Pure Imagination: An Experiment in Reading" offers what Strandberg calls "an explanation and vindication of Warren's own purpose and practice in poetry."[18] This essay on Coleridge served as a catalyst that defined a whole range of themes and concerns that appear in Warren's later poetry, fiction, and criticism. For Warren, poetry and life were inextricably linked, and his intense study of Coleridge and the English Romantics in preparation for this essay resulted in a form of "conversion" experience that shaped his spiritual outlook as well as his aesthetic philosophy. While this "conversion" was not quite as dramatic and sudden as Paul's transforma-

17. Robert Penn Warren, "An Interview in New Haven with Robert Penn Warren," by Richard B. Sale, in *Talking with Robert Penn Warren*, ed. Watkins et al., 130.

18. Strandberg, *Poetic Vision*, 31. The text of Warren's "A Poem of Pure Imagination: An Experiment in Reading" used in subsequent references is taken from *SE*, 198–305.

tion on the road to Damascus, it did signal a definite shift in the attitudes and approaches of Warren's work. Through a series of developments that evolved throughout Warren's career, the Eliotic dissatisfaction of Warren's early poems and the despairing naturalism of *Night Rider* give way to the qualified yet definable joy of *Audubon: A Vision* and the hesitant hopefulness of *A Place to Come To*. The specter of the ruined garden never disappears from Warren's fictive or poetic world, but the poetry written after his drought embodies a distinctly Romantic prospect of renewal and a capacity for joy largely absent from his earlier work.

Samuel Taylor Coleridge proved to be the poet most influential in the early stages of Warren's Romanticism. Even prior to his intensive examination of the Romantics in preparation for writing "A Poem of Pure Imagination," Warren refers in "Pure and Impure Poetry" (1942) to Coleridge's theory of the tripartite relationship between poetry, the reader, and the world. According to Warren, a poem—a good poem—"must, as Coleridge puts it, make the reader into an 'active creative being.'"[19] For the most part, Warren keeps to the intrinsic task of poetry, offering his famous statement that "poetry wants to be pure, but poems do not" (*SE*, 4). The emphases on "irony," "metrical variation," and "shifts in tone or mood" signal Warren's concurrent involvement with the New Critics, but his reference to Coleridge's theory of poetry moves his discussion outside of the insularity of poetry into the area of poetic effect. Warren's brief but telling mention of Coleridge foreshadows the central issue of "A Poem of Pure Imagination": poetry, far from being irrelevant to life, "brings the whole soul of man into activity," offering truth and meaning through "a sacramental conception of the universe" (*SE*, 229).

In his preface to the Modern Library edition of *All the King's Men*, Warren mentions that his writing of the novel was "interrupted . . . by the study for and writing of a long essay on Coleridge." This essay, "A Poem of Pure Imagination," offers Warren's interpretation of *The Rime of the Ancient Mariner* within the context of two dominant

19. Robert Penn Warren, "Pure and Impure Poetry," in *SE*, 27.

themes: the Coleridgean sense of "the One Life within us and abroad" and, in Warren's words, the "story of crime and punishment and repentance and reconciliation" (*SE*, 214). Apart from Warren's famous and still controversial commentary on the structural organicism of the *Rime* and his insistence on seeing the text as "pure" or "self-contained," he also examines the way Coleridge joins a Christian mythos with the aesthetic theme of imaginative power. By associating the "pure imagination" with a larger spiritual context, Warren develops his argument that Coleridge's great Romantic poem reinforces the connection between poetry and the world. At the same time, Warren is able to provide his own statement about the nature of poetry, of life, and the relationships between them.

Throughout Coleridge's *Rime*, Warren finds "a final fusion of the imagination and the sacramental vision" (*SE*, 248). In Warren's reading of the poem, the Mariner shoots the albatross, thus committing a crime, or sin, against God and nature. The Mariner then, according to Warren, "suffers various pains, the greatest of which is loneliness and spiritual anguish; upon recognizing the beauty of the foul sea snakes, experiences a gush of love for them and is able to pray; is returned miraculously to his home port, where he discovers the joy of human communion in God, and utters the moral, 'He prayeth best who loveth best,' etc." (*SE*, 222). Warren defines the theme of the Mariner's fable as "the notion of universal charity . . . the sense of the 'One Life,' in which all creation participates" (*SE*, 222). This "One Life," a phrase Warren takes from Coleridge's "The Eolian Harp" ("O the one life within us and abroad, / Which meets all motion and becomes its soul"), has primarily religious overtones, but combined with the aesthetic theme of the imagination, as Warren asserts, it achieves dimensions beyond an orthodox reading.[20]

In Warren's discussion of the *Rime*, he argues that the theme of the "One Life" illustrates the Romantic belief in the inextricable nature of religion and poetry. The imagination provides the integral key

20. Samuel Taylor Coleridge, "The Eolian Harp," in *Samuel Taylor Coleridge: A Critical Edition of the Major Works*, ed. H. J. Jackson (Oxford: Oxford University Press, 1985), 28.

to discovering the "One Life," and Warren maintains that the power of the imagination "presents us with the 'great forms' of nature, but those forms as actively seized upon by the human mind and loved *not merely as vehicles for transcendental meaning but in themselves as participating in the reality which they 'render intelligible'*" (original emphasis) (*SE*, 249). Such an alliance between religion and poetry was ultimately Coleridge's goal, a "glorious synthesis in which all breaches would be healed and all malice reconciled." Referring to both the *Rime* and Coleridge's philosophical prose works, Warren argues that the Romantic poet's chief aim was to develop "some vital connection between them [poetry and religion]." Coleridge was certainly not alone in this need to establish the relationship between truth and poetry. As Warren points out, other Romantic poets such as Blake, Wordsworth, Shelley, and Keats "felt that they had to justify their existence," and this justification rested upon the claim that "poetry gives truth" (*SE*, 251). Warren acknowledges that the "problem of truth and poetry" was by no means first recognized by the English Romantics, but for them, in an age of scientific positivism and utilitarianism, this issue "was not only a constant topic for criticism, but was, directly or indirectly, an obsessive theme for poetry itself" (*SE*, 250).

This "obsessive theme," as his own poetry verifies, is ultimately Warren's chief concern as well, and in "A Poem of Pure Imagination" he gives formal and objective expression to some of his most deeply felt intuitions and ideas about poetry. He is at his weakest in his discussion when he attempts to assign particular referents to the symbols in the poem, and critics such as Elder Olson, E. E. Bostetter, and William Empson reacted to "A Poem of Pure Imagination" with something akin to savagery. However problematic the details of Warren's analysis appear, this essay is exceptional not only for the close reading and critical appreciation it yields concerning Coleridge's poem but also for the insight it affords into the development of Warren's poetic philosophy. From his Fugitive days until the end of his career, the art of poetry remained Warren's central focus, despite his early "drought" and the perception of the reading public that he was primarily a novelist, due in part to the success of his 1946 novel *All the King's Men.* However, to consider and announce oneself as a poet first and foremost leaves one vulnerable to the spotlight of modern critical and public scrutiny, a fact Warren knew full well from his Romantic predecessors. He was not a man inclined to excesses of any kind, political or otherwise, but he lucidly and eloquently sustained a defense of the importance of poetry and offered observations and treatises on this subject from the 1940s until the end of his career in the 1980s.

In "Pure and Impure Poetry," "A Poem of Pure Imagination," "Knowledge and the Image of Man," and *Democracy and Poetry,* Warren examines the tenuous predicament of poetry (and the arts in general) in the modern world. "Knowledge and the Image of Man" offers Warren's most direct and articulate reconsideration of Shelley's classic formulation in "A Defence of Poetry," which asserts that "poetry marries exultation and horror, grief and pleasure, eternity and change; it subdues to union . . . all irreconcilable things."[21] Warren had first referred to "Defence of Poetry" in "A Poem of Pure Imagination," citing Shelley's claim that poetry "'is at once the centre and circumference of knowledge,'" and he explicitly singles out Shelley's ideas regarding the "the socializing function of the imagination" (*SE,* 255). In "Knowledge and the Image of Man," Warren advances his personal creed that "poetry—that is, literature as a dimension of the creative imagination—is knowledge." Echoing Wordsworth's assertion in the 1800 Preface to *Lyrical Ballads* that "poetry is the breath and finer spirit of all knowledge,"[22] Warren extends his Romantic correlative into a reconciliation of opposites, submitting his view that poetry joins "the ugly with the beautiful, the slayer with the slain,

21. Shelley, "A Defence of Poetry," in *Shelley's Poetry and Prose,* ed. Reiman and Powers, 505. Warren's essay "Knowledge and the Image of Man" originated as an address given at a conference on the unity of knowledge during Columbia University's bicentennial celebration in 1954. Warren turned this general philosophical topic into his own defense of poetry; the address was later published in *Sewanee Review* [3 (spring 1955): 182–92].

22. William Wordsworth, *Selected Poems and Prefaces by William Wordsworth,* ed. Jack Stillinger (Boston: Houghton Mifflin, 1965), 456.

what was known as shape now known as time, what was known in time now known in shape, a new knowledge. It is not a thing detached from the world but a thing springing from the deep engagement of spirit with the world" ("Knowledge," 61). Warren calls this "deep engagement of spirit with the world" an "osmosis of being," a concept parallel to the "One Life" theme he had explored in Coleridge's *Rime*. Like the Romantics, Warren maintains that poetry provides the individual with a means of exploring his "continual and intimate interpenetration" with the world.

While Harold Bloom contends that Shelley is "a poet not much to Warren's taste," Warren clearly endorses the basic premises of Shelley's "Defence."[23] Whatever reservations Warren may have had about Shelley's politics, he firmly aligns himself with Shelley's aesthetic views. Shelley felt compelled to respond to Thomas Peacock's satirical account of the decline of poetry because of his uncomfortable realization that the view that Peacock had only half-jokingly assumed was very similar to that actually held in his day by Utilitarian philosophers and material-minded laymen who either openly reviled or contemptuously ignored the imaginative faculty and its achievements. Warren perceived similar threats to the creative imagination within his own time, particularly in the aftermath of the New Deal, which he saw as encouraging "Common Man-ism" at the expense of the right "to define ourselves in a communal aspiration" ("Knowledge," 57). Although Warren concedes that such a menace to the "Right to Knowledge" varies from period to period (often masked in the guise of concern for the public good), he takes a decidedly Romantic position on poetry's importance to the individual as well as society.

The "Right to Knowledge," Warren asserts, has its roots in Christian theology, and using the Christian myth of the Fall and the expulsion from Eden as his guiding metaphor, he submits his vision of redemption through knowledge: "Man can return to his lost unity, and if that return is fitful and precarious, if the foliage and flower of the

23. Harold Bloom, "Sunset Hawk: Warren's Poetry and Tradition," *Modern Critical Views: Robert Penn Warren*, ed. Harold Bloom (New York: Chelsea House, 1986), 201.

innocent garden are now somewhat browned by a late season, all is the more precious for the fact, for what is now achieved has been achieved by a growth of moral awareness. The return to nature and man is the discovery of love, and law. But love through separateness, and law through rebellion. Man eats of the fruit of the Tree of knowledge, and falls. But if he takes another bite, he may get at least a sort of redemption. And a precious redemption" ("Knowledge," 186). Like Wordsworth's fallen persona in the "Intimations Ode" and "Tintern Abbey," Warren contends that the redemptive unity with nature—albeit "a sort of redemption"—offers man a "unity presupposing separateness," or, to quote Wordsworth, "a sense sublime / Of something far more deeply interfused." But similar to his analysis of Coleridge's *Rime*, Warren's use of religious associations serves not as an elucidation of a particular doctrine or orthodoxy but instead reinforces the human effort toward knowledge and the truths implicit in the reconciliation of moral with aesthetic concerns. Twenty years later, in *Democracy and Poetry*, Warren again takes up his defense of poetry, confronting the modern (although by no means novel) assumption that artistic creativity has little value for society as a whole.

Democracy and Poetry, Warren's most thorough and evocative exploration of poetry and its relation to modern society, stands near the end of his career as the summation of observations taken from a lifetime of steady contemplation. Furthermore, *Democracy and Poetry* afforded Warren the opportunity to address what he saw as a cultural crisis in twentieth-century America by applying the Romantic principles that he had been exploring indirectly in his poetry and fiction or directly in his nonfiction essays. In this work, Warren, like Shelley before him, regards the creation of poetry and fiction as the antidote for the dissociated self: "The self has been maimed in our society because, for one reason, we lose contact with the world's body, lose any holistic sense of our relation to the world, not merely in that there is a split between emotion and idea but also because perception and sensation are at a discount—except when set off from the fullness of life and marketed as sensationalism" (*DP*, 73). Although Warren shunned the political extremism of a revolutionary like Shelley, he

agreed unequivocally with Shelley's denunciation of an acquisitive society seemingly bent on the obliteration of all not practical or, in
Warren's words, "vendible" (*DP*, 68).

Whether Warren intended *Democracy and Poetry* as a direct and
deliberate twentieth-century response to Shelley's "A Defence of
Poetry" is questionable, but he does specifically refer to Shelley's concern that poetic imagination has outrun the individual's "conception"
in an age of science and technology. In the lectures that comprise *Democracy and Poetry*, Warren addresses what he calls "the interrelation
of three things: democracy, poetry (really art in general), and selfhood" (*DP*, xi). With the use of the word "democracy," Warren
places his remarks within the context of the Western world, with
America as his point of reference. In particular, he examines a persistent threat that disturbed Shelley a century and a half earlier—the
decline of poetry and the arts in the face of expanding technology,
overt materialism, and an apathetic public.

In "A Defence of Poetry," Shelley declares that "the cultivation of
poetry is never more to be desired than at periods when, from an ex-
cess of the selfish and calculating principle, the accumulation of the
materials of external life exceed the quantity of the power of assimi-
lating them to the internal laws of human nature. This sentiment
finds a twentieth-century American voice, as Warren argues in *Democracy and Poetry*, that "in the face of the increasingly disintegrative
forces in our society, poetry may affirm and reinforce the notion of
the self" (*DP*, 42). Wordsworth, in direct parallel to Shelley, indi-
cated that poetry was never more needed "than at the present time,"
when the brunt of "great national events" and "the uniformity of . . .
occupations" attendant upon "the increasing accumulation of men in
cities" tend to reduce the mind "to a state of savage torpor." The "savage torpor" that Wordsworth observed in his age ominously portends
what Warren sees as the great social problem of the twentieth century, "that of maintaining the mental and emotional stability of a
pampered and purposeless mass and of lulling it from violence" (*DP*,
83). Warren shared with the English Romantics the notion that
poetry could serve as an "antidote . . . for passivity" and a means of
reinvigorating the self as an entity involved in time and the world.

For Warren, Shelley's assertion that "man, having enslaved the elements, remains himself a slave" takes on special urgency in modern America, and what began for Warren as the project of affirming the intrinsic merit of poetry evolved into a lifelong examination of the relationship between literature and culture.[24] In all of these concerns, the Romantics provided Warren with the vision that guided his aesthetic and spiritual concerns, and as I explore in the following chapters, his poetry as well as his fiction reveals how powerfully the Romantic influence affected his approach to his craft.

Establishing influence is always difficult, especially since most truly great writers absorb other great writers' ideas and transform these echoes into distinctive, personalized voices. What I hope this book will encourage is the consideration of Robert Penn Warren's work within a continuity of literature and thought. Warren died in 1989, leaving behind some of the most insightful and provocative poetry and prose written in the twentieth century. James Dickey classified Warren among those poets who can "give you a sense of poetry as a thing of final importance to life." The "final importance," as the evolution of his poetry reveals, suggests questions, not solutions. John Stuart Mill wrote in his *Autobiography* that reading Wordsworth's poetry "saved" him from "dejection" and opened his eyes and mind to "the excitement of beauty": "What made Wordsworth's poems a medicine for my state of mind, was that they expressed, not mere outward beauty, but states of feeling, and of thought coloured by feeling. . . . In them I seemed to draw from a source of inward joy, of sympathetic and imaginative pleasure, which could be shared by all human beings."[25] The "sympathy" of human understanding—at its best, redemption, at its worst, complicity—emerges as the central

24. Shelley, "A Defence of Poetry," in *Shelley's Poetry and Prose*, ed. Reiman and Powers, 503; Wordsworth, *Selected Poems and Prefaces*, ed. Stillinger, 449; Shelley, "A Defence of Poetry," in *Shelley's Poetry and Prose*, ed. Reiman and Powers, 503.

25. James Dickey, "In the Presence of Anthologies," *Sewanee Review* 66 (spring 1958): 308; John Stuart Mill, *Autobiography* (London: Oxford University Press, 1924), 125.

theme of Warren's best works. Even if Warren were not "saved" by reading the Romantics (as Mill claimed to have been), they certainly offered him a timely utterance in the midst of personal crisis and creative drought. When Warren asks in *Audubon*, "what / Is man but his passion?" (*CP*, 254), he speaks of himself. Because of this passion, he exemplifies the type of artist the Romantics celebrated. Perhaps, in the end, this belief that the passion of art and the passion of life are inextricable enabled him to walk in the world as well as love it.

I

Romantic Confluences and Eliotic Strains

Like many aspiring poets in the 1920s, Robert Penn Warren began his poetic career under the commanding influence of T. S. Eliot and the Modernists. When Warren arrived at Vanderbilt University in 1921, he found himself in a vital and thriving artistic community.[1] In a 1953 interview Warren recalled that "writing poetry was almost epidemic at the university, and even an all-Southern center on the football team did some very creditable lyrics of a Housmanesque wistfulness."[2] When new issues of the *Nation* or the *Dial* appeared with poems by Hart Crane, Yeats, or Eliot, the copies sold out immediately. The 1922 publication of *The Waste Land* sparked a passion for experimentation in poetic techniques, and Warren and many of his classmates not only emulated Eliot's style but could also recite the poem by heart. *The Waste Land* so captivated the young Vanderbilt undergraduate that he decorated the walls of the dormitory room that

1. Warren commented to William Ferris in a 1979 interview, "It's very funny how a little isolated place like Vanderbilt knew more about modern poetry and art than places like Harvard or Berkeley" (Ferris, "Robert Penn Warren," 127).

2. Warren, "A Self-Interview," interview by Newquist, in *Talking with Robert Penn Warren*, ed. Watkins et al., 2.

he and Allen Tate shared with scenes from Eliot's poem. Even many years later, Tate could vividly describe the murals of the typist putting the record on the gramophone and the rat creeping through the vegetation.

In a 1967 interview, Warren told Roy Newquist that "every Southern freshman, literarily inclined, knew *The Waste Land* by heart in 1922." Later, in a 1972 reminiscence, he emphasized how deeply this formidable poem had affected him: "[*The Waste Land*] was certainly a watershed in my life and the lives of many of my friends. It came out in November, 1922, in the *Dial* magazine. That's where I first read it. I was completely overwhelmed by it and didn't, I promise you, understand it at all. . . . But my generation—we memorized the poem and went around quoting it all the time."[3] Warren's exposure to Eliot's poetry during his undergraduate years at Vanderbilt had a profound and lasting effect on his own poetry, particularly his earliest lyrics. As Warren's career progressed, his poetry underwent a continuous series of stylistic and thematic mutations, never resting for long within one particular technical form or attitude. Much of the critical attention concerning Warren's poetic development concentrates on his "drought" of the 1940s and the ways his poetry in the aftermath of this period evinces certain shifts in style and tone. Thus the tendency has been to divide Warren's poetry into two phases: "early" Warren, the poetry characterized by the apparent strains of Eliotic influence in both method and theme; and "late" Warren, the poetry distinguished by his movement toward the direct, the personal, the visionary, and above all, the Romantic.

I see far more continuity of development than this division allows. The evolution of what I refer to as Warren's "Romantic vision" does not necessarily entail a complete break with the early influence of Eliot. It may appear odd to align Warren's emergent Romanticism with a figure who, according to George Bornstein, "worked to purge literature as a whole of the contamination of Romanticism," but as

3. Warren, "Conversation with Eleanor Clark and Robert Penn Warren," interview by Newquist, *ibid.*, 88, and "Robert Penn Warren," interview by Walker, *ibid.*, 148.

Bornstein's analysis of Eliot's works reveals, the latter "became a leading anti-Romantic theorist even while covertly resuscitating high Romantic modes and developing poetry whose true theme is his alternate fascination with his own imagination and his fear of it."[4] Warren began writing poetry under the authority of the High Moderns, who in turn were struggling to free themselves, by an anti-Romantic reaction, from the influence of nineteenth-century Romanticism. Although the evolution of Warren's distinctive poetic voice depended on his gradual independence from the early and commanding influence of Eliot, his development as a poet and a writer rested not on a complete rift with Eliot but rather on the incorporation of Eliot's latent Romanticism within his own emerging Romantic vision.

In several respects the patterns of Eliot's and Warren's long careers involve a connection to the Romantics. Although Eliot emerged as an anti-Romantic modern during the height of his poetic and critical career, a thorough understanding of Eliot's literary career begins at what Bornstein calls "its neglected beginning, in his obsession with the Romantic poets." Both Eliot and Warren were influenced early by the Romantic poets (as a young man and during his course work at Vanderbilt, Warren had read Byron, Wordsworth, Blake, Keats, Shelley, and Coleridge), but in his twenties Eliot vehemently rejected the Romantics, associating them with immaturity, loss of control, and unbridled and destructive passion. One might speculate that Eliot came to view the Romantics as figures representing his own puerile adolescent longings. In *The Use of Poetry and the Use of Criticism* (1933), Eliot recalls that he "was intoxicated by Shelley's poetry at the age of fifteen" but later found it "almost unreadable."[5]

---

4. George Bornstein, *Transformations of Romanticism in Yeats, Eliot, and Stevens* (Chicago: University of Chicago Press, 1976), xii. According to Bornstein, "[Eliot's] rapprochement coincided with his emergence as a dramatist, Christian sociologist, and institution; in none of these identities did the Romantics threaten him, and in some of them Coleridge was a positive help."

5. *Ibid.*, 95; T. S. Eliot, *The Use of Poetry and the Use of Criticism: Studies*

Eliot's three stages of poetic growth—childhood, adolescence, and maturity—trace in many ways the pattern of Warren's development, but Warren's "mature" poetry takes a decidedly different course than Eliot's. In "On the Development of Taste," Eliot writes that "in childhood we enjoy rousing ballads and battle poetry." True to this example, the young Warren did enjoy such poetry as a boy, citing in several interviews his fond memories of learning "Horatius at the Bridge" and "How They Brought the Good News from Ghent to Aix": "I thought [they were] pretty nearly the height of human achievement. I didn't know whether I was impressed by riding a horse that fast or writing the poem. I couldn't distinguish between the two, but I knew there was something pretty fine going on." Warren also comments that reading "Lycidas" at age thirteen changed forever his perception of poetry: "By that time I knew it wasn't what was happening in the poem that was important—it was the poem. I had crossed the line."[6] But we must remember that Warren entered Vanderbilt at age sixteen, barely out of adolescence, and there he discovered Eliot, Pound, and the Metaphysical poets of the seventeenth century.

Eliot equates his own "adolescent" phase of poetic growth with his reading of the Romantics. At fourteen, he read Edward FitzGerald's *The Rubáiyát of Omar Khayyám:* "It was like a sudden conversion; the world appeared anew, painted with bright, delicious, and painful colours. Thereupon I took the usual adolescent course with Byron, Shelley, Keats, Rossetti, Swinburne . . . but we must not confuse the intensity of the poetic experience in adolescence with the intense experience of poetry." Bornstein argues that Eliot correlated his early literary passions with the onset of sexuality, with Romanticism later becoming the "scapegoat for the sins of his poetic youth and sirens of his early maturity."[7] Warren, in contrast, came under the influence of Eliot

---

in the Relation of Criticism to Poetry in England (Cambridge: Harvard University Press, 1961), 88.

6. Eliot, *The Use of Poetry and the Use of Criticism*, 33; Robert Penn Warren, "Warren on the Art of Fiction," interview by Ralph Ellison and Eugene Walter, in *Talking with Robert Penn Warren*, ed. Watkins et al., 28.

7. Eliot, *The Use of Poetry and the Use of Criticism*, 33–34; Bornstein, *Transformations*, 106.

himself at roughly the same age that Eliot claimed to have undergone a "sudden conversion" to the Romantics. Eliot repudiated the Romantics as part of his struggle to form his independent identity as a poet; only in his later years did he reach an incomplete reconciliation. Owing in significant measure to Eliot's anti-Romantic criticism, John Crowe Ransom downplayed the Romantics' contribution to literature and emphasized instead the type of poetry that the developing New Criticism explored, that of the seventeenth century. Warren, however, even under the tutelage of Ransom, never dissociated himself from Romantic poetry or philosophy. The poetry Warren produced from his Vanderbilt days until *Selected Poems, 1923–1943* conveys not only his willingness to explore new ways of modulating the styles encouraged by his mentors but also his ever-growing need to express the visionary hope rooted in his sense of being in the world.

Far from a discontinuity, Warren's evolution toward Romanticism fulfilled the growing needs of his poetic career. Eliot, however, may have repressed his Romantic leanings out of fear that the Wordsworthian sense of "spontaneous emotion" would compromise his desire for aesthetic and spiritual order. His embrace of orthodox religion kept at bay the "daemonic inner forces" that he felt the Romantic theory of the imagination unleashed.[8] Bernard Bergonzi speculates that "[Eliot] regarded poetic creation as a possibly dangerous and even sacrificial surrender to unknown forces. Thus described, Eliot's poetic seems unexpectedly Romantic."[9] This emphasis on the primacy of the poetic imagination suggests Eliot's aesthetic kinship with what is perhaps the central tenet of Romantic theory, but unlike the Romantics, rarely does Eliot project the imagination as a unifying

---

8. Eliot, *The Use of Poetry and the Use of Criticism*, 26.

9. See Bornstein, *Transformations*, and Bernard Bergonzi, *T. S. Eliot* (New York: Macmillan, 1972), 72. Regarding the differences in attitude and personality between Eliot and Warren, Calvin Bedient (*In the Heart's Last Kingdom: Robert Penn Warren's Major Poetry* [Cambridge: Harvard University Press, 1984], 7) points out that "because he [Warren] was really much happier than Eliot ever was to be a creature of this world . . . his true manner had to be earthier than his mentor."

or stabilizing force. One might argue that *The Four Quartets* presents such a vision, but as Bornstein and Bergonzi propose, Eliot's reconciling "vision" in these poems ultimately depends upon a defined orthodox Christian tradition. But Warren, turning an unblinking eye toward the power of the imagination, could not rest easily in the surrender of self that orthodoxy implied. The conflict between naturalism and what Warren came to call "the religious sense" became his most dominant theme as his career progressed, and issues of personal faith and aesthetic crisis tested Warren severely as an individual and as a poet. At a crucial point in his life, the Romantics offered him the vision that made such new definitions possible.

During his undergraduate years at Vanderbilt, Warren's introduction to the works of Eliot was furthered by Allen Tate, whose knowledge of French Symbolism and Modernism made him a capable guide and critic. Six years Warren's senior (he had entered the university late while Warren had entered early), Tate engaged Warren in passionate conversations about art and poetry, encouraged him to join the Fugitive group, and acted as a mentor and critic for the younger poet's early endeavors. As roommates, Warren and Tate exchanged ideas about each other's poetry, even editing each other's work at the typewriter as the other one slept. Warren considered Tate the "most modern" of the Fugitive group, and Tate readily acknowledged Eliot as his poetic "master." Yet perhaps because of his youth or because of his temperament, or perhaps even because of the two men's differing socio-geographic backgrounds, Warren did not embrace Eliot's Modernism to the extent that Tate did. Cleanth Brooks argues that Warren "never suffered from any anxiety of influence," and "not even his older and much venerated poet friends, like John Crowe Ransom and Allen Tate, ever really pulled Warren into their orbit," although in a letter written during the early days of their friendship, Warren told Tate, "I am content for the moment at least, and you should be happy for a bright disciple."[10]

10. Cleanth Brooks, "Afterword," *Southern Quarterly* 31, no. 4 (summer 1993): 107; Louise Cowan, *The Fugitive Group: A Literary History* (Baton Rouge: Louisiana State University Press, 1959), 150.

Eliot's immediate impact is evident in Warren's earliest published poems. Warren's 1923 poem "Crusade," one of his first poems published in the *Fugitive*, attests to the influence that the recently published *Waste Land* had on his poetic technique.[11] In this poem Warren alludes to the quest-romance recounted by Crusaders after the collapse of Jerusalem:

> We have not forgot the clanking of grey armors
> Along the frosty ridges against the moon,
> The agony of gasping endless columns,
> Skulls glaring white on red deserts at noon;
> Nor death in dank marshes by fever.
>
> (*CP*, 3–4)

Images of Eliotic decay and sterility appear throughout the poem, and the tone conveys a sense of doubt similar to the spiritual anguish in *The Waste Land* as well as Eliot's earlier poems, especially in the line, "Can rock and dust presage a fabled heaven?" (*CP*, 4). Although the persona hopes for "yonder promised peace," he questions the possibility of transcendence amidst the "rock and dust" (*CP*, 4). The glory of the cause he has embarked upon seems remote in the face of physical annihilation ("Flies on bloated bodies rotting by the way") (*CP*, 3), and in his despair the speaker anticipates the "opiate of forgetfulness" that death brings (*CP*, 4).

Warren's next submission to the *Fugitive* in August 1923, "After Teacups," reads like an amalgam of voices from several of Eliot's poems, especially "Gerontion" and "The Love Song of J. Alfred Prufrock." The deliberate echoes of these poems manifest Warren's talent at appropriating Eliot's use of the composite speaker, a representative voice that moves backward and forward in time and encompasses mythical and historical frames of reference. The unnamed speaker in Eliot's "Gerontion" states,

---

11. The excerpts from the *Fugitive* appeared in the June–July 1923 and August–September 1923 issues.

I was neither at the hot gates
Nor fought in the warm rain
Nor knee deep in the salt marsh, heaving a cutlass,
Bitten by flies, fought[12]

Warren's speaker in "After Teacups" expresses a similar frustration at trying to find meaning in an elusive, collective memory of past failure: "I was not on the parapets at Cretae / Dreading sails black against the low red moon, / When my ruin overthrew me / Nor did it claim me with the plunge of Grecian spears (*CP*, 4–5)."[13] The second stanza's opening lines, clearly modeled on the beginning of Part V of *The Waste Land*, also invoke the sense of historical downfall: "After shouting and trumpets and the crash of splintering lances, / After these and weeping." As Marshall Walker observes, "The effect here is sarcastic, the speaker evoking grand possibilities only as a preface" to his later revelation of present inadequacies.[14] Using one of Eliot's dominant techniques, Warren juxtaposes scenes from antiquity with the present to signify modern man's detachment from the ideological and emotional intensity of the past.

In Warren's next *Fugitive* poem, "Midnight," the tone shifts, introducing another speaker whose gestures and poses remind us of J. Alfred Prufrock:

Your gaunt uncomprehending eyes
Clutch at me as I start to rise
Rattling my newspaper, saying 'It is late.'
You draw the pins, release your flood of hair.
Am I doomed to stand thus ever,
Hesitating on the stair?[15]

12. T. S. Eliot, *Collected Poems, 1909–1962* (New York: Harcourt Brace Jovanovich, 1963), 29.

13. In a letter to Donald Davidson in September 1926, Warren referred to the "obvious and wavering experimental quality" of "After Teacups" and "Midnight." See Marshall Walker, *Robert Penn Warren: A Vision Earned* (New York: Harper and Row, 1979), 7on.

14. *Ibid.*, 53.

15. Robert Penn Warren, "Midnight," *Fugitive* 2 (October 1923), 142.

Warren composed "Crusade," "After Teacups," and "Midnight" as a trilogy of monologues, and the three poems combine to produce the superimposition of the remote past and the empty present, a device characteristic of Eliot's early poems. While these monologues are, at best, Warren's skillful manipulation of methods practiced by Eliot, they contain little of the rich natural imagery that appears in Warren's later poetry. In this period of intense imitation, Warren adopted Eliot's cosmopolitan settings and characters for his poems, producing such lines as "But dissolution clutched me / Descanting at Mme. Atelie's salon / Of balls at Nice and coursing at L'Enprix" (*CP*, 5). While these poems reveal much technical competence, in retrospect they appear strained and contrived. As a direct model, the urbane sophistication of Eliot's poetry seems startlingly remote from the experiences of an eighteen-year-old boy from a small town in Kentucky. Yet as Warren gained skill and confidence, he abandoned the particulars of Eliot's poetic situations in favor of his own forms and subjects. While he continued to use themes and images that were reminiscent of Eliot, particularly the primary theme of the modern "dissociated sensibility," Warren experimented with other modes and explored the possibilities of both lyrical and narrative structures.

Even though Eliot's poetry represented one strain of aesthetic form and practice in the 1920s, the revival of the seventeenth-century Metaphysical poets was in large part also Eliot's doing. Warren's two mentors at Vanderbilt provided him with guidance in both modes: Tate introduced Warren to the experimental verse of the Modernists, and John Crowe Ransom advocated the model of the well-made poem, the conscious artifact whose power lay in its structure as well as its tropes. An apt pupil, Warren produced poems in the Metaphysical vein Ransom admired while exploring the modern dissociated sensibility in the poetry of Eliot and Pound. In Tate, Warren observed how the modern theme of alienation could be adapted to southern landscapes and history. From Ransom, he absorbed the ways in which the technical resources of conventional forms could be modulated to accommodate a variety of styles and voices. James Justus has observed that "Warren managed better than any other of his Southern contemporaries, perhaps including Ransom, to write the kind of poetry that most of them admired and wrote about." In

The Metaphysical Passion: Seven Modern American Poets and the Seventeenth-Century Tradition, Sona Raiziss credits Warren for his skill at blending both the Metaphysical and Modernist modes, noting that "Warren's critical contemplation of modern man's predicament in general still gives him room to utilize his particular surroundings for color and detail."[16] With Ransom as his enthusiastic guide to the Metaphysical poets and Tate as his mediator to the Moderns (both in varying degrees paying the highest homage to Eliot), Warren devoted his energies early on to crafting poems that offered a combination of both modes.

The ten-year period between Warren's graduation from Vanderbilt in 1925 and the publication of his first collection of poems in 1935 was amazingly full; he pursued his graduate studies at Berkeley, Yale, and Oxford and then went on to serve as an assistant professor at Southwestern College in Memphis (now Rhodes College), Vanderbilt University, and Louisiana State University.[17] During this time he also published *John Brown: The Making of a Martyr* (1929) and completed a B.Lit. dissertation at Oxford (1930). In the early 1930s he contributed the essay "The Briar Patch" to the Agrarians' published collection of essays *I'll Take My Stand* and, with Cleanth Brooks and Charles Pipkin at LSU, founded the influential journal the *Southern Review*. Although he directed much of his energy during the 1930s toward teaching and other projects, all the while he continued to write poems. His diligence resulted in his first volume of poetry, *Thirty-Six Poems*, published by Alcestis Press in 1935.

With the exception of "To a Face in the Crowd," the works in *Thirty-Six Poems* are the products of Warren's post-Vanderbilt years. From the tightly compressed formality of "Letter of a Mother" and "Problem of Knowledge" to the Eliotic moods and landscapes of

16. See Justus, *Achievement*, 50, and Sona Raiziss, *The Metaphysical Passion: Seven Modern American Poets and the Seventeenth-Century Tradition* (Philadelphia: University of Pennsylvania Press, 1952), 196.

17. The best source of information on this period in Warren's life is Joseph Blotner's long-awaited biography on Warren (*Robert Penn Warren: A Biography* [New York: Random House, 1997]).

"Kentucky Mountain Farm" and "The Return: An Elegy," the poems in this collection bear the mark of Warren's apprenticeship under Ransom and Tate and evoke comparisons to Eliot as well as to Marvell and Donne. "The Return" and "Kentucky Mountain Farm" are the most derivative of Eliot, but even the explicit borrowings are aimed toward original effect, demonstrating Warren's ability to adapt many of Eliot's themes and stylistic devices to his own distinctive explorations of selfhood, mortality, and time.

In "The Return," the speaker is trapped in an anguished vision of time and death, although as Victor Strandberg observes, "Unlike Eliot, Warren dispenses with side issues like ethics and culture. . . . No Prufrocks or Sweeneys or indiscreet typists can distract this speaker."[18] Images of sterility and spiritual frustration recur throughout the poem, but unlike the multivoiced *Waste Land*, "The Return" has only one speaker, and the context is much more focused and specific. The speaker is apparently traveling home to pay a final visit to his dying mother, and this event in turn supplies the narrative framework for his meditations. The poem opens with a line obviously influenced by Part V of *The Waste Land* ("a damp gust bringing rain"), but in Warren's poem the speaker's interior "waste land" is transposed into the pine-filled Kentucky woods:

> The east wind finds the gap bringing rain:
> *Rain in the pine wind shaking the stiff pine.*
> Beneath the wind the hollow gorges whine.
> The pines decline.
> Slow film of rain creeps down the loam again
> Where the blind and nameless bones recline.
>
> (*CP*, 33 [original emphasis])

These bones, "conceded to the earth's absolute chemistry," are all that remain of human existence, thus reducing life to nothing more

---

18. Victor Strandberg, *A Colder Fire: The Poetry of Robert Penn Warren* (Westport, Conn.: Greenwood Press, 1965), 9.

than "calcium phosphate lust speculation faith treachery" (*CP*, 33). This naturalistic position renders a view of human existence as insignificant and transitory, and external nature offers no support or answer—the pines surrounding the graveyard only "snore" and "lurch beneath the thunder's livid heel" (*CP*, 33). Such an outlook is evident in Eliot's early poetry, especially in *The Waste Land* ("I will show you fear in a handful of dust"), and much of the imagery invites comparison to Eliot's theme of spiritual barrenness. But in Warren's poem, the shifts in levels of consciousness belong to one speaker, the grieving son, and his contemplations are inextricably fixed within the confines of his individual circumstance and memory. Unlike Eliot's characters, such as Prufrock or the speaker in "Gerontion," Warren's speaker has a past and a particularized present.

The placement of the speaker within a singular context is one of the ways that Warren deviates from Eliot's use of characterization. At the beginning of the poem, the speaker's meditations resemble those of Tiresias, perhaps the most prominent figure in the array of juxtaposed voices in *The Waste Land*. In his notes to that poem, Eliot explains that Tiresias is "the most important personage in the poem," yet he is a "mere spectator": "What Tiresias sees, in fact, is the substance of the poem." Hugh Kenner asserts that Tiresias represents a "generic Eliot character . . . the name of a possible zone of consciousness where the materials which he is credited with being aware of can exist."[19] The figure of Tiresias undergoes a conspicuous transformation in Warren's poem. No longer is this observer "blind, throbbing between two lives"—he is "not blind" ("Eyes, not blind, press to the Pullman pane / Survey the driving dark and silver taunt of rain") (*CP*, 33). He is painfully aware of his role not as an experienced observer (in *The Waste Land*, "And I Tiresias have foresuffered all . . .") but as a novitiate to the world of time and decay. The speaker asserts, "I have a name," and part of the burden of this "name" rests in his nec-

19. Eliot, *Collected Poems*, 65; Hugh Kenner, "Bradley," in *T. S. Eliot: A Collection of Critical Essays*, ed. Hugh Kenner (Englewood Cliffs, N.J.: Prentice-Hall, 1962), 36–37.

essary confrontation with what this identity means regarding the death of his mother and, inevitably, the death of self.

The voice yearning for meaning that appears many years later in *Audubon: A Vision* ("Tell me the name of the world") makes a brief appearance in "The Return" *("tell me its name") (CP,* 258), but in this phase of Warren's career, the prospects of reconciling the external world and time with the internal search for significance appear grim. The speaker instead turns to sardonic dissatisfaction, mocking the values of human ritual:

> give me the nickels off your eyes
> from your hands the violets
> let me bless your obsequies
> if you possessed conveniently enough three eyes
> then I could buy a pack of cigarettes
>
> *(CP,* 33)

Even the presence of the violets, much like the hyacinths offered in *The Waste Land,* serves as nothing more than a reminder of "fear in a handful of dust." The speaker in Warren's poem, seeking to escape the burden of time and experience, chants a nursery rhyme in a senti-mental mantra of regression: "turn backward turn backward o time in your flight / and make me a child again just for tonight" *(CP,* 34).[20] The speaker's wish for escape into an idealized childhood signifies his desire to deny the facts of his immediate present, but the concluding line of this wish ("good lord he's wet the bed come bring a light") implies that such escapism is ultimately futile.

The most significant reminder of Eliot's influence in this poem comes near the end, as the speaker seeks spiritual sustenance to com-bat his grief. Certainly, the landscape offers no solace, for even the wind reminds him of the cruel reduction of human life: "the old bitch is dead / what have I said! / I have said only what the wind said /

20. This line originally appears in Elizabeth Akers Allen's lullaby "Rock Me to Sleep" (1860).

wind shakes a bell the hollow head" (*CP*, 33). The contemplation of history also forces the speaker back to naturalistic despair: "a hundred years they took this road / . . . the hungry people the lost ones took their abode / . . . here is the house the broken door the shed" (*CP*, 34). Faced with external as well as internal bleakness, Warren's speaker wrestles with his inability to find adequate blessing for himself and his mother:

> I cannot pluck
> Out of this land of pine and rock
> Of red bud their season not yet gone
> If I could pluck
> (In drouth the lizard will blink on the hot limestone)
>
> (*CP*, 34–35)

The speaker recalls the biblical commandment, "Honor thy father and mother in the days of thy youth," which reinforces his awareness of indebtedness to the past and his family, but even this honor appears hollow, "for time uncoils like the cottonmouth" (*CP*, 35).

Similar to Eliot's "The Fire Sermon," Warren's poem alludes to the lines "O Lord Thou pluckest me out / O Lord Thou pluckest" from St. Augustine's *Confessions*. Yet unlike Eliot's reference to Augustine's prayer, which denotes salvation provided by an external source, Warren's speaker turns inward to the self. He knows he cannot be "plucked" out of his predicament. Instead, he voices a desperate wish to "pluck" from within himself the capacity for cathartic grief:

> If I could pluck
> Out of the darkness that whirled . . .
> Could I stretch forth like God the hand and gather
> For you my mother
> If I could pluck
> Against the dry essential of tomorrow

To lay upon the breast that gave me suck
Out of the dark the dark and swollen orchid of this sorrow.

(*CP*, 35)

Many of the images, cadences, and allusions to Christian theology, combined with the theme of the frustrated soul surrounded by spiritual barrenness, reveal Eliot's influence. However, Warren's reference is local, individual, and personal, creating what Marshall Walker deems a more "immediate if not permanent" effect.[21] The exploration of memory and time would become the crux of Warren's mature poetry: he examines not only the emptiness caused by cultural decay (although that, too, is one of Warren's most significant concerns) but also the deeply personal effects of estrangement from the past and the self.

Further evidence of Eliot's influence in *Thirty-Six Poems* appears in "Kentucky Mountain Farm," a segmented collage rife with many of the same themes and images that appear in "The Return."[22] Like the latter poem, "Kentucky Mountain Farm" may dispense with the decadent, urban locales scattered throughout *The Waste Land*, but the alienated speaker in Warren's poem still must contend with the naturalistic desolation of the "tortured and reluctant rock" (*CP*, 36). With its seven divided sections designated by titles and Roman numerals, "Kentucky Mountain Farm" appears to be deliberately patterned after *The Waste Land*. The parallels between the two begin with the very first lines of Warren's poem: "Now on you is the hungry equinox" (*CP*, 35). Here, as in Eliot's poem, the coming of spring ("April is the cruellest month") serves only to remind the "little stubborn people of the hill" of their thwarted and dormant passions. Similar also to Eliot's "Gerontion," the arrival of springtime signals the return of a de-

21. Walker, *A Vision Earned*, 61.

22. The original version of "Kentucky Mountain Farm," which appears in *Thirty-Six Poems* and *Selected Poems, 1923–1943*, contains seven sections; in *New and Selected Poems, 1923–1985*, the poem has been cut to five sections, omitting Parts IV and V, "The Cardinal" and "The Jay." I will be referring to the original text with its seven sections.

vouring Christ ("In the juvenescence of the year / Came Christ the tiger"), but in Warren's poem, the only inkling of the external comes in the ceaseless rhythms of birth and death,

> The season of the obscene moon whose pull
> Disturbs the sod, the rabbit, the lank fox,
> Moving the waters, the boar's dull blood,
> And the acrid sap of the ironwood.
>
> (*CP*, 35)

The lifeless rocks, secure in their "sweet sterility," become a "rebuke" to the creatures that must bend to the tyranny of natural function.

As bleak as the landscape of "Kentucky Mountain Farm" may appear, within this poem are hints of a theme that later emerges as an integral element of Warren's developing Romanticism. In section II, "At the Hour of the Breaking of the Rocks," Warren temporarily alleviates the naturalistic harshness of the preceding section by introducing the "spirit [which] moves and never sleeps . . . that held the foot among the rocks, that bound / The tired hand upon the stubborn plow, / Knotted the flesh unto the hungered bone" (*CP*, 36). This "spirit," while suggestive of the Christian God that Eliot invokes in "Ash Wednesday," does not seem to be a clearly orthodox vision of divine presence. Rather, it appears as Warren's version of a spiritual unity from which all emanates and to which all returns, reminiscent of Coleridge's "One Life" theme as well as Wordsworth's compelling sense of unity in "Tintern Abbey." Warren's resistance against a purely naturalistic reduction of human significance gives the speaker of this poem, at least briefly, an inkling of the self within time. The images in this poem of the "Down shifting waters" and the "tall, profound / Shadow of the absolute deeps" (*CP*, 36) resonate throughout much of Warren's later poetry, accentuating his insistence that looking into the abysses of time, however futile the attempt may seem, will ultimately yield at least a subjective notion of one's purpose and identity. The speaker does not envision the intimations of immortality that Wordsworth speaks of, but in this early phase of Warren's poetic career we can begin to hear the voice of the "yearner" striving to discover a dimension whereby the self may be redeemed from annihilation.

The threat of annihilation, however, is persistent and ever present, and in section III the speaker must contend with the frightening notion of bodily cessation: "There are many ways to die / Here among the rocks in any weather" (*CP,* 36). The allusions to *Waste Land* in this section ("Here is no water but only rock / . . . If there were water we should stop and drink / Amongst the rock one cannot stop or think") appear to place the "spirit [which] moves and never sleeps" in the realm of the impersonal, leaving death as the only means of achieving unity. The image of the "body, naked and lean / . . . tumbling and turning" recalls Eliot's Phlebas the Phoenician, and the effect of this image renders death peaceful and desirable:

> Think how a body, naked and lean
> And white as the splintered sycamore, would go
> Tumbling and turning, hushed in the end,
> With hair afloat in waters that gently bend
> To ocean where the blind tides flow.
>
> (*CP,* 36)

Note the similarities to Eliot's Phlebas:

> Phlebas the Phoenician, a fortnight dead,
> Forgot the cry of gulls, and the deep sea swell
> And the profit and the loss.
>   A current under the sea
> Picked his bones in whispers. As he rose and fell
> He passed the stages of his age and youth
> Entering the whirlpool.[23]

In a world seemingly devoid of meaning, death offers the cessation of activity and thought. Eliot's "whirlpool" and Warren's "blind tides"

23. Eliot, *Collected Poems,* 72n. Strandberg discusses in great detail the similarities between Warren's speaker in "Kentucky Mountain Farm" and Eliot's Phlebas; see *A Colder Fire.*

symbolize the rhythms of nature, cycles of life and death in which all humans take part. Warren's image is evocatively beautiful but not very comforting—like the sycamore swept away by "a creek in flood," human life becomes just another natural phenomenon subject to arbitrary destruction.

The abstract, mythologized depiction of "a way to die" then gives way to the more immediate impact of history. The "other ways" to die include war, specifically the Civil War:

> In these autumn orchards once young men lay dead—
> Gray coats, blue coats. Young men on the mountainside
> Clambered, fought. Heels muddied the rocky spring.
> Their reason is hard to guess, remembering
> Blood on their black moustaches in moonlight.
> Their reason is hard to guess and a long time past:
> The apple falls, falling in the quiet night.
>
> (*CP,* 37)

Like the alienated speaker in Allen Tate's "Ode to the Confederate Dead," Warren's speaker also feels estranged from the past, unable to relate to the purpose that led the young soldiers to their deaths. The ideals and issues of history may appear irrelevant in the face of naturalistic reduction, but the repetition of the line "Their reason is hard to guess" suggests that the speaker cannot easily assume that the soldiers' motives, like the apple "falling in the quiet night," are devoid of moral content.

In "The Cardinal" and "The Jay," the fourth and fifth sections of "Kentucky Mountain Farm," Warren turns from the issues of human history and struggle. He presents images of natural beauty that act as counterforces to the "lean men" who must labor with and against nature. In the manner of the Romantic reverie, the speaker admires the cardinal and its "vision of scarlet devised in the slumberous green" (*CP,* 37). Although Warren would not incorporate such imagery in full force until later in his career, the cardinal becomes a symbol, like Keats's nightingale, of eternal beauty. Unaware of time and death, the cardinal appears to embody the spontaneous joy of existence and can even partake of its own immortality:

> Here is a bough where you can perch and preen
> Your scarlet that from its landscape shall not fade,
> Lapped in the cool of the mind's undated shade,
> In a whispering tree, like cedar, evergreen.
>
> (*CP*, 37)

The jay of section V, while "flagrant and military," embodies much the same sense of joy, but it reminds the speaker of the passage of time and the movement of "the truant sun." The jay's noisy insistence "stops an old fellow trudging the first snow, / As once the boy who with his dog and gun / Followed the rabbit's track long ago . . ." (*CP*, 37). While the jay may be a "Bright friend of boys," it is also a "troubler of old men," making the speaker aware of his capitulation to time and death. Both the cardinal and the jay, untroubled by the search for identity, evoke the speaker's inchoate longing for merger with nature. Although such a merger is unattainable, the birds symbolize the human desire for transcendence. For Warren, the desire in itself is significant because it sustains the search for meaning.

Perhaps the most important bird imagery appears in the sixth section of "Kentucky Mountain Farm," entitled "Watershed." Here we encounter the image of the "sunset hawk" that appears often in later poems as Warren's most dominant and personal symbol of the imagination. In this poem, according to Marshall Walker, the hawk balances the "rebuke of the rocks" by offering a lesson in humility and exposing the speaker "as deficient in joy, in the capacity to live in time, and in the faculty of vision."[24] The speaker stands upon the highest peak available (the "watershed"—from this high place all things flow") and observes the hawk as

> . . . His gold eyes scan
> The crumpled shade on gorge and crest

24. Walker, *A Vision Earned*, 47.

> And streams that creep and disappear, appear
> Past fingered ridges and their shriveling span.
> (*CP*, 38)

Humbly, the speaker then returns to his vision of human frailty that must take its "rest" "Under the broken eaves." For the residents of this "waste land," "Not love, happiness past" motivates their actions, but only a sort of weary "certitude" (*CP*, 38). The nobility, vision, and joy that the hawk signifies appear separate and remote from the ennui of human existence.

At the end of "Kentucky Mountain Farm," in "The Return" (a section of the poem, not to be confused with "The Return: An Elegy"), the speaker urges his "backward heart" to summon his "vagrant image" again, but "The tree, the leaf falling, the stream, and all / Familiar faithless things would yet remain / Voiceless" (*CP*, 38). The search for ultimate reality merely brings the speaker inward, back to his isolated self, and the "return" implied in the title of this section is marked by disappointment and loss—the speaker's "own image, perfect and deep / And small within loved eyes, had been forgot" (*CP*, 39). Even though the poem ends on this sorrowful note, there is at least the intimation of a "buried world . . . lost / In the water's riffle or the wind's flaw" (*CP*, 39). The speaker apprehends the perfect self-fulfillment enacted in the natural world, yet his self-consciousness—the barrier between the human self and the natural world—prevents him from obtaining the ideal unity he desires.

"The Return: An Elegy" and "Kentucky Mountain Farm" represent two of Warren's most skillful manipulations of Eliot's imagery and techniques. "To a Face in the Crowd," the concluding poem, also presents the same proliferation of rock and water images and, as in the other two poems, phrases reminiscent (at times too familiar) of several Eliot poems. The central theme that unites "To a Face in the Crowd" with the other works in *Thirty-Six Poems* is the question of man's ability to exist on a purely naturalistic level, an issue that Warren addresses (with varying results) throughout his poetry and novels. Structurally, "To a Face in the Crowd" reveals the influence of Ransom as well as Eliot. The traditional four-line, iambic pentameter stanzas and the mannered archaisms signify Warren's ambition to create the "well-made" poem in the seventeenth-century manner that both Eliot and Ransom advocated. The imagery and emergent themes, however, reveal the most noticeable influence of Eliot. Although the speaker leaves his addressee anonymous, he does acknowledge the familiarity of the "face": "In dream, perhaps, I have seen your face before."[25] Whether the "Brother" is another person or a reflection of the speaker himself, the "face" represents the totality of human ancestry, "the children of an ancient band / Broken between the mountains and the sea" (*CP*, 61).

As a part of "an ancient band," the speaker feels a sense of estrangement that is both individual and collective. The speaker, like his "Brother," must pass "among the rocks" where "the faint lascivious grass / Fingers in lust the arrogant bones of men" (*CP*, 61). The presence of these rocks, reminiscent of the barren landscapes in "Kentucky Mountain Farm" and "The Return: An Elegy," signifies the "monument" of the past, particularly the codes of the fathers, in which the "children" must try to find significance. In his various analyses of Warren's poetry and fiction, Randolph Runyon has emphasized the signs by which the conflicts between fathers and sons (fathers literal or symbolic) come to light, and he sees "the tall taciturn stone, / Which is your fathers' monument and mark" (*CP*, 61) as indicative of "the text he [the father] leaves behind for the son to decipher." The image of the "taciturn tall stone" in Warren's poem is remarkably similar to Eliot's stone images in "The Hollow Men": "Here the stone images / Are raised, here they receive / The supplication of a dead man's hand."[26] The same lost souls desperately striv-

---

25. In his first novel, *Night Rider*, published just four years before the publication of *Thirty-Six Poems*, Warren uses the image of the "face in the crowd." During his speech at a political rally, Percy Munn focuses upon "a man of about fifty, wearing faded blue overalls and a straw hat," realizing "with a profound force that that man was an individual person, not like anybody else in the world" (*NR*, 25).

26. Randolph Runyon, "Repeating the 'Implacable Monotone' in *Thirty-Six Poems*," *Mississippi Quarterly* 48, no. 1 (winter 1994–95): 56; Eliot, *Collected Poems*, 80.

ing for meaning inhabit both poets' rocky landscapes, "weary nomads" in the midst of broken icons of the past.

In Eliot's "The Hollow Men" and Warren's poem, both poets evaluate the cultural and spiritual crisis in modern civilization, but with Warren's use of the word "nomads," the crisis relates to individual alienation as well. In this sense, "To a Face in the Crowd" also resembles "The Love Song of J. Alfred Prufrock," especially when the speaker mourns, "I was afraid—the polyp was their shroud. / I was afraid" (*CP*, 61). The anxiety the speaker expresses suggests the sense of inadequacy, not necessarily in the face of human indifference but in the shadow of the "fathers' monument and mark." Warren's speaker must continue his journey, an individual sufferer in the midst of other sufferers:

> Your face is blown, an apparition, past.
> Renounce the night as I, and we must meet
> As weary nomads in this desert at last,
> Borne in the lost procession of these feet.
>
> (*CP*, 61)

Like Eliot's crowd flowing over London Bridge in *The Waste Land* ("I had not thought death had undone so many"),[27] Warren's "lost procession" contains similar wanderers, other "faces" searching for meaning in the "desert." The speaker and the "brother" he addresses have no choice but to confront the dark history they both share: "A certain night has borne both you and me." The only communion possible arises from their recognition of a common past, and part of that legacy is the naturalistic fate in which all humans participate.

Throughout *Thirty-Six Poems*, Warren repeatedly questions man's ability to find meaning in the face of deterministic forces, and in an essay published four years after this first volume of poetry, he poses the question directly and credits Eliot with the most profound treatment of the issue of naturalism. In his contribution to a *Kenyon Re-*

27. Eliot, *Collected Poems*, 55.

view series of essays entitled "The Present State of Poetry," he claims that the "work of Eliot probably provides the most important single influence on American poetry." On one level, Warren seems to be affirming the qualities of his own poetry that are most derivative of Eliot: "Most of the direct imitations of Eliot now seem to have been undertaken without a real comprehension of his central theme. On the one hand, the imitations tended to be merely imitations of the obvious features of his style directed to concerns more or less remote from his; or imitations on the other, based on a naive misreading of his essential position, a misreading which defined him as a poet of 'despair,' a poet who was presenting a romantic nostalgia, a contrast between a degenerate present and a noble past."[28] What Warren considers as Eliot's "great importance for contemporary poetry" is the "contemplation of a question which is central in modern life": "Can man live on the purely naturalistic level?"

This very question is the dominant focus of *Thirty-Six Poems* as well as of Warren's next volume, *Eleven Poems on the Same Theme*, and although he does not apply his evaluation of Eliot's influence to himself, the parallels are obvious. In "The Present State of Poetry," Warren alludes to an earlier *Kenyon Review* essay in which Philip Rahv had divided American poets into two groups, the "palefaces" and the "redskins." Warren argues that despite the "redskin" poets' rejection of Eliot on the grounds that his poetry represents "a retreat from life, a refusal to consider the social situation, and a self-indulgent individualism," much in Eliot corresponds to their philosophy: "They saw a world without sustaining faith, a world of fragments, and if they did not accept Eliot's specific prescription, they accepted his general one."[29] Eliot's "general" prescription, as Warren sees it, is based on "the brotherhood of man, a myth of redemption and regeneration." While neither a true "redskin" nor a "paleface" (although he would exhibit tendencies much more aligned with the

---

28. Robert Penn Warren, "The Present State of Poetry: III. In the United States," *Kenyon Review* 1 (autumn 1939): 395.

29. Philip Rahv, "Paleface and Redskin," *Sewanee Review* (Premiere issue, 1939): 251–56; Warren, "The Present State of Poetry," 396.

"redskin" group as his career progressed), Warren insightfully points
out how elements of Eliot's poetry might be assimilated into a poet's
"essential direction." Warren's "essential direction" as a poet owes
much to the influence of Eliot, and although strains of this influence
never entirely disappear, *Eleven Poems on the Same Theme* displays his
ability to apply his own "prescription"—not necessarily a remedy but
at least a diagnosis—to the problems of time, identity, and human fate.

Eleven Poems on the Same Theme appeared in 1942 as one of the
"Poet of the Month" series published by New Directions. The relatively slim volume contained a few poems Warren wrote while at
Louisiana State University, but the majority were products of his
time in Italy and Mexico. Reviewers responded to this collection with
generous and often lavish praise: *New York Times* critic Peter Munro
Jack lauded Warren as "something of a Donne in the twentieth century," and Louis Untermeyer commented admiringly in the *Yale Review* on the lyrical power of Warren's new poetry.[30] Numerous critics
(many in retrospect) have argued that *Eleven Poems* represents Warren's steady movement away from early influences, particularly from
Eliot, but in direct and indirect ways, the poems in this collection
reflect the strains of Eliot embedded in Warren's emerging, original
voice.

In *Eleven Poems*, Warren further develops his use of personal and
subjective history, his experimentation with verse pattern, and his
frequent employment of the "you" of direct address. Echoes of Eliot's
themes are still present, but the situations and scenes are less imitative, more insistent in their need to uncover some meaning outside of
purely naturalistic considerations. Warren tentatively approaches the
possibility of some sort of redemption in several of these poems, especially in "Revelation," in which the young boy who has "spoken
harshly to his mother" learns the lesson that "In separateness only
does love learn definition" (*CP,* 71). But separateness prevails more

30. Peter Munro Jack, review of *Eleven Poems on the Same Theme,* by
Robert Penn Warren, *New York Times Book Review* 26 (April 1942): 4, and
Louis Untermeyer, "Cream of the Verse," review of *Eleven Poems on the Same
Theme,* by Robert Penn Warren, *Yale Review* 32 (winter 1943): 366.

often than love, and the search for the unacknowledged self introduces Warren's speakers to hidden and sometimes destructive distur-
bances beneath the surface of the conscious self.

Several critics have offered their interpretations of the "Same
Theme," which unites the poems in the volume. Strandberg, using
Jung's model of the repressed unconscious self, sees this theme as
Warren's exploration of undiscovered identity. W. P. Southard, in
"The Religious Poetry of Robert Penn Warren," reads the poems in
this collection as "prayers" for "participation, knowledge, and love."
Similarly, F. O. Matthiessen asserts that Warren's dominant theme
is "his protest against the tendency of our scientific age to reduce
knowledge to abstraction, and to rob experience of its religious tension by making sin meaningless."[31] Directly or indirectly, each critic's
explanation of the "Same Theme" draws us back to Warren's question in "The Present State of Poetry": "Can man live on a purely naturalistic level?" The answer is resoundingly "no" throughout *Eleven
Poems*, but the poems themselves suggest that living (or rather, finding meaning in living) involves taking on the burden of discovering
one's place within both subjective and objective time, within one's
construct of self and the world that inherently shapes the self. Thus
the "Same Theme" that emerges in *Eleven Poems* is ultimately an
added dimension to Warren's earlier theme of naturalism: like Frost's
question of "what to make of a diminished thing,"[32] Warren looks at
the fragmentary nature of experience and suggests how, by assem-
bling these fragments, we might learn "Something important about
love, and about love's grace" (*CP*, 71).

The first three poems display Warren's use of the complicated
symbolism and imagery characteristic of the Metaphysical mode. In
"Monologue at Midnight," the specific experiences of hearing a

31. See Strandberg, *A Colder Fire*, and *Poetic Vision*. See also W. P.
Southard, "Speculation I: The Religious Poetry of Robert Penn Warren,"
Kenyon Review 7 (autumn 1945): 653–76, and F. O. Matthiessen, "American
Poetry Now," *Kenyon Review* 6 (autumn 1944): 683–96.

32. Robert Frost, "The Oven Bird," in *Complete Poems of Robert Frost*
(New York: Holt, Rinehart and Winston, 1964), 150.

hound baying and watching a flame's reflection transform into a contemplation of issues outside the immediacy of ordinary human time. The concrete nature of experience moves into the realm of the abstract, similar to Donne's use of physical objects to embody meaning beyond their literal significance. The speaker in "Monologue at Midnight" asks,

> The hound, the echo, the flame, or shadow . . .
> And which am I and which are you?
> And are we Time who flee so fast,
> Or stone who stand, and thus endure?
>
> (*CP*, 65)

Being neither "Time" nor "stone," the speaker is unsure of his identity and must contend with the loss of "joy and innocence." This loss points toward the crucial issue that underlies *Eleven Poems on the Same Theme*: does time render all things meaningless? The naturalistic crisis of "Monologue at Midnight" seems to suggest that isolation and guilt are the inevitable products "of earth and of our pleasure," part of the "mathematic" of simple existence. Although the speaker recalls how "we" once participated "In joy and innocence," the poem is a "monologue," a sole speaker enveloped in solipsistic isolation. The "integers of blessedness" appear elusive, and "the poor deluded cock / Salutes the coldness of no dawn" (*CP*, 65). Warren's version of the "dark night of the soul" offers little hope for a return to the original state of innocence described at the beginning of the poem, but the speaker's need to define the self marks his awareness of the cleavage between the self and others as well as between the self and time.

Love and death, timeless subjects in themselves, were the favorite subjects of the Metaphysicals, and like Eliot, Warren addresses these aspects of human experience with the added urgency of modern alienation. Since time brings loss, the desire to remain fixed and motionless is tempting, like the scene presented in "Bearded Oaks." In what Justus calls "an impeccable updating of Marvell," "Bearded Oaks" portrays two lovers who lie suspended in a state of marine-like velleity "Beneath the languorous tread of light" (*CP*, 65), retreating into complacency instead of acting upon the awareness of mortality.[33] Warren's lovers, detached from the world of sense and time, passively lie on the ocean-bottom of existence ("Twin atolls on a shelf of shade"), where the "storm of noon" cannot touch them. "Passion and slaughter, ruth, decay" (*CP*, 66) sift like sediment through the murk of their inertia:

> All our debate is voiceless here,
> As all our rage, the rage of stone;
> If hope is hopeless, then fearless fear,
> And history is thus undone.
>
> (*CP*, 66)

But as we know from Warren's continued exploration of the past (especially in *Brother to Dragons*) history is never "undone," despite any attempts to detach oneself from responsibility and action. The end of the poem reminds us that any retreat can only be temporary:

> We live in time so little time
> And we learn all so painfully,
> That we may spare this hour's term
> To practice for eternity.
>
> (*CP*, 66)

The assurance of mortality ("The caged heart makes iron stroke") appears to be the only aspect of life worth contemplating, thus any consideration of love becomes merely a matter of sterile sameness. The sense of peace the lovers experience is illusory and transitory. Unlike the "still moments" of Warren's later poetry, this preserved moment of stasis allows no vision beyond a contemplation of death.[34]

33. Justus, *Achievement*, 50.

34. The lovers' "perfect" immobility hints at a similar conclusion reached by Eliot in the last lines of "Burnt Norton," the first poem in *Four Quartets*: "Ridiculous the waste sad time / Stretching before and after" (*Collected Poems*, 181).

"Picnic Remembered" extends the theme of isolation presented in "Bearded Oaks," with the speaker and his companion (the same two lovers?) resting "among the painted trees," buried beneath "the amber light." As the speaker and his companion lie unmoving and passive, the present stillness seems to render the past insignificant:

> . . . that all we had endured
> Seemed quaint disaster of a child,
> Now cupboarded, and all the wild
> Grief canceled; so with what we feared.
>
> (*CP,* 66)

Warren again employs a metaphysical conceit to describe the speaker's resistance to time and change, but his alteration of Donne's or Marvell's use of the conceit pointedly marks how insufficient this temporary escape is against the "darkness" of life within time. In "The Canonization," Donne's speaker compares himself and his lover to two flies, "made such by love," but Warren's lovers are "Twin flies . . . as in amber tamed, / With our perfections stilled and framed / To mock Time's marveling after-spies" (*CP,* 67). Not passion but fear of motion and of time keeps these lovers locked in their resigned postures.

The harmony and purity of this static image is, as the speaker realizes, a "bright deception," because "The darkness on the landscape grew / As in our bosoms darkness, too." On one level, the speaker's awareness recalls Wordsworth's conception of the darkened vision that comes with maturity and experience, but the speaker in Warren's poem struggles with the notion of finding "abundant recompense" from this visionary diminution. The "Joy . . . from the region happier mapped," which sustained the speaker and his companion in the past, appears inaccessible to the "hearts, like hollow stones," suggestive of Eliot's "Hollow Men," who can ascertain no hope in their present circumstances; they are "Shape without form, shade without colour, / Paralysed force, gesture without motion." Warren's speaker longs for the innocence of the past and wonders if the exile from the Eden of youth and love signifies the permanent loss of any significance in life:

> Or are we dead, that we, unmanned,
> Are vacant, and our clearest souls
> Are sped where each with each patrols
> In still society, hand in hand,
> That scene where we, too, wandered once
> Who now inherit new province,
> Love's limbo, this lost under-land?
>
> (*CP*, 67)

This "paradise lost" has its own Miltonic echoes, especially in the allusion to Adam and Eve's departure from Eden: "They, hand in hand, with wand'ring steps and slow, / Through Eden took their solitary way."[35] But unlike Milton's account of the Fall, which offers the hope of salvation by the future coming of Christ, Warren's alienated couple has no guarantee of redemption.

Just as the failure to maintain the "visionary gleam" of the past signals the inability to find meaning in the present, "The then, the now" become cenotaphs, like a monument erected for a person whose body has been lost. But hope is not entirely extinguished, and the speaker's question at the end of the poem suggests a possibility for redemption more akin to Wordsworth's philosophy than Milton's: "Or is the soul a hawk that, fled / On glimmering wings past vision's path / Reflects the last gleam to us here" (*CP*, 67). The image of the hawk, so frequently used by Warren as a symbol of imaginative vision, represents in this poem a glimpse of the transcendence afforded to earthbound humans "Though sun is sunk and darkness near." There is little indication here or even in Warren's later poetry that "Uncharted Truth's high heliograph" (*CP*, 67) will ever be fully revealed to human consciousness, but in "Picnic Remembered" we find the tentative probings that would later emerge as the primary focus of Warren's poetry: how the "gleam" apart from the external darkness of naturalism and the inner darkness of isolation can at least lead to the limited "blessedness" obtainable within life and time.

35. John Milton, *Complete Poems and Major Prose*, ed. Merritt Y. Hughes (New York: Macmillan, 1957), 469.

The next poem, "Crime," depicts a scene quite different from the static "peace" in the first three poems. The subject of this poem, a murderer who flees the scene of his crime and "lies in the ditch and grieves," seemingly lacks the guilt and repression that haunts the speakers in the preceding poems. Whereas the speaker in "Bearded Oaks," for example, retreats from the world, the "mad killer" in "Crime" thrusts himself into the world, but in either case, inaction or action, the outcomes are the same. Both represent evasion, flights from the self that result in denial or violence. But why are we to "Envy the mad killer"? Because at least he acts, "though in error," and at least what he has buried "under the leaves" can be discovered, unlike "that bright jewel you have no use for now" (*CP*, 68), the hidden aspect of the self that has been either rationalized away or simply buried beneath the conscious self. As this poem suggests, an awareness of self by necessity includes an awareness of the capacity for evil, something the mad killer acknowledges but the "you" of the poem refuses to accept:

> Peace, all he asked: past despair and past the uncouth
> Violation, he snatched at the fleeting hem, though in error;
> Nor gestured before the mind's sycophant mirror,
> Nor made the refusal and spat from the secret side of his mouth.
>
> (*CP*, 68)

Warren's ironic invitation for us to "Envy the mad killer" thus becomes an indictment of the "you" in the poem, "for what he has buried is buried / . . . nor is ever known / To go on any vacations with him, lend money, break bread" (*CP*, 68). As the next poem, "Original Sin: A Short Story," discloses, simply denying evil does not free one from complicity or guilt.

Although "Original Sin: A Short Story" is placed in the middle of *Eleven Poems*, it was actually composed later than any of the other poems in the volume. First appearing in *Kenyon Review* in the spring of 1942, this poem marks a significant departure from Warren's early poetry. After the strict verse patterns and controlled tone of "Bearded Oaks" and "Picnic Remembered," "Original Sin: A Short Story" is less confined by conventional forms, and the tone becomes increasingly more personal as Warren intensifies the "you" of direct address. The title itself points toward the parallels Warren saw between a universalized Christian myth and the individualized fall and redemption, linking original sin with the dark, nightmare self that the consciousness would prefer to ignore.

In a broad sense, the central theme of "Original Sin" resembles Eliot's accounts of moral acedia and the implications of man's "fallen" nature. Eliot's exploration of the tensions between sin and redemption, however, finally turns toward the progression from nihilistic despair to spiritual enlightenment through religious conversion. Bornstein points out that "Eliot's own conception of Christianity rested on original sin," and in a 1930 essay on Baudelaire, Eliot argues that "what really matters is Sin and Redemption." Eliot, like Warren, continually addresses throughout his career the difficulty of apprehending the significance of life in an external world seemingly bent on reducing humans to "fractured atoms" (a phrase Eliot uses in "Gerontion" and that Warren later borrows for "Kentucky Mountain Farm"). Warren, however, avoids defining "redemption" in terms of a preformed orthodox tradition. As Justus points out, "Warren is too much the secular poet to believe that intimations about man's fragile and uncertain meaning can be dissolved in the certain acid of God's grace."[36] Whereas Eliot's baptism into the Anglican Church in 1927 attested to his willingness to accept orthodox Christianity, Warren sought a mode of belief that would allow him to assess his spiritual concerns without the limitations of a particular theology. With their emphasis on the unification of moral and aesthetic concerns, the Romantics offered Warren an alternative to the devoutly religious stance that Eliot had assumed.

Warren's essay on Coleridge was pivotal in establishing not only his critical regard of the Romantics but also his connections between what he calls "the moral or religious concern and the aesthetic con-

---

36. Bornstein, *Transformations*, 119. T. S. Eliot, "Baudelaire," in *Selected Essays* (New York: Harcourt, Brace and World, 1964), 378–79. Justus, *Achievement*, 4.

cern" (*SE*, 253). Although Warren did not publish "A Poem of Pure Imagination: An Experiment in Reading" until 1945, there is evidence that he had begun his formal study of the Romantics several years earlier, primarily during his work on *Understanding Poetry* with Cleanth Brooks. Prior to his lengthy treatment of Coleridge's *Rime of the Ancient Mariner*, Warren had written little on Romantic poetry. Yet in "Pure and Impure Poetry" (1942), he refers to Coleridge and Shelley as poetic models, especially in their conceptions of poetry as a means to make the reader into "an active creative being" (*SE*, 27). Unlike Eliot (who despite his avowed dislike of Romantic poetry viewed Coleridge's criticism as valuable), Warren found much in the Romantic philosophy that was akin to his own poetic practice. Thematically, "Original Sin" forecasts the treatment that Warren would later give to Coleridge's *Rime*. Although this poem seems about as far as one can get from Eliot's early depictions of urban monotony or his later abstract monologues on the nature of faith and doubt, in many ways "Original Sin" parallels the Romantic principles that Eliot had expressed indirectly in his poetry. The division of self and the arduous journey toward redemption, both themes of the Romantic tradition, appear throughout Eliot's poetry, but the way in which Eliot resolves these conflicts through religious doctrines sets him apart from the Romantics. Warren, in contrast, unfolds a "short story" of original sin that incorporates religious associations with a more secularized, psychological effort to reconcile the secret self with the conscious self.

"Original Sin" offers a fable of what Justus calls "the unitary nature of nature." In Warren's reading of the *Rime*, the Mariner's recognition of his kinship with the sea snakes not only offers him a redemptive unity with nature but also affirms his complicity with the deepest and most despised elements of nature. Although the albatross that the Mariner shoots is associated with innocence (Coleridge describes it as "the pious bird of good omen"), it is as much a part of the "sacramental vision of the universe" as the sea snakes, the "despised creatures of the calm."[37] Only after recognizing that the sacred

---

37. Justus, *Achievement*, 54; Samuel Taylor Coleridge, *The Rime of the Ancient Mariner*, in *Samuel Taylor Coleridge*, ed. Jackson, 54.

and the despised are related in dynamic fusion can the Mariner free himself of the weight of the albatross. Symbolically, both elements of nature, the "pious" bird as well as the "despised creatures of the calm," constitute two poles of being, innocence and experience. Yet it is not innocence that "redeems" the Mariner. His partial redemption comes with the blessing of what he has deemed corrupt and "Other." The albatross sinks "Like lead into the sea" only after the Mariner discovers love, but love through separateness and rebellion. Significantly, Coleridge's poem does not end with the blessing of the sea snakes: the Mariner carries the burden of his guilt with him always. Through his compulsive storytelling, he reminds his reluctant listener that the lesson of his experience cannot be escaped or ignored.

Similarly, as the speaker in "Original Sin" reminds us, "Oh, nothing is lost, ever lost! at last you understood" (*CP*, 69). Thus we also arrive in Wordsworth's territory: intimations of immortality dependent on the rediscovery of a hidden self. But the self that is hidden in "Original Sin" is closer to Coleridge's conception of a presupposed self. It does not "trail clouds of glory" but instead "fumble[s] at your door before it whimpers and is gone" (*CP*, 69). In Warren's poem, the conscious, social self tries to repress the specter of the buried self, even though the "nightmare" is harmless and unsure, like an imbecilic child:

It tries the lock. You hear, but simply drowse:
There is nothing remarkable in that sound at the door.
Later you may hear it wander the dark house
Like a mother who rises at night to seek a childhood picture;
Or it goes to the backyard and stands like an old horse cold in the pasture.

(*CP*, 70)

Warren's vision of original sin in this poem appears only vaguely menacing; in fact, it seems quaintly pathetic and helpless. The specter threatens to disrupt the speaker's carefully preserved construct of self, but it is a minor annoyance: "It acts like the old hound that used to snuffle at your door and moan" (*CP*, 69). The images of the old hound, the grandfather with his "wen . . . / Which glinted in sun like rough garnet" (*CP*, 69), the mother "who rises at night to seek a childhood picture," and the old horse "cold in the pasture" (*CP*, 70) are all domestic and familiar, but they, too, are a part of "original sin," those repressed elements that the conscious self would like to intellectualize away.

Warren's depiction of the undiscovered self in this poem blends two seemingly disparate Romantic themes: Coleridge's belief in original sin and Wordsworth's conception of original innocence and unity. Although his temperament and philosophy aligned him more with Coleridge, Warren explores Wordsworth's idea of primal sympathy. By incorporating Coleridge's theme of human complicity, Warren takes an unflinching look at the loss of "innocence" in both religious and psychological terms, and how, once reconciled to this loss, the individual can achieve a "new definition" of wholeness. Since in "A Poem of Pure Imagination" Warren sees the blessing of the sea snakes as the Mariner's moment of redemptive unity, it is not surprising that in "Original Sin," the speaker can come to terms with the undesirable part of the self only by recognizing its inherent connection to the persona that inhabits "Harvard Yard," the surface self.

As John L. Stewart observes, Warren defines original sin "according to his ontological premises": "In Warren's work man does evil because he does not have enough self-knowledge to avoid it, and he always will since complete self-knowledge is impossible to obtain."[38] Many of the speakers in Warren's early poems express a resigned acceptance of such limitations, although not without resistance. While Eliot writes in "Little Gidding" that "Sin is Behovely," a necessary condition of humanity, the progression from doubt to faith through the *Four Quartets* suggests that Eliot's vision of redemption depends on spiritual surrender. What Eliot saw as the unregenerate impulses threatening the spiritual order of self Warren saw as the force that drives man toward knowledge, leading to the mixed blessing presented in "Original Sin." For Warren, and for his Romantic counterparts, the separation of idea from nature through abstraction or doc-

---

38. Stewart, *The Burden of Time*, 538.

trine could only inhibit knowledge, thus creating a condition of passive estrangement rather than an awareness of moral and communal responsibility.

This awareness that the world is "all of one piece" (*AKM*, 188), a realization that Warren later develops in Jack Burden's struggle toward knowledge in the novel *All the King's Men*, emerges as the central theme of "Terror," the concluding poem in *Eleven Poems*:

> Not picnics or pageants or the improbable
> Powers of air whose tongues exclaim dominion
> And gull the great man to follow his terrible
> Star, suffice . . . .
>
> (*CP, 77*)

Rather, the "you" of the poem is "born to no adequate definition of terror," and the only understanding of terror available is "like a puppy, darling and inept" (*CP, 77*). Written while Warren was in Italy from 1939 to 1940 on a Guggenheim fellowship, "Terror" documents a specific period of history, yet although the rise of Fascism and imminent war appear to be the central issues, the internal battlefield becomes the dominant subject of exploration.

As Warren explains in the 1951 *Modern Poetry*, the epigraph to "Terror" is from a press release that he had read in the daily newspaper in Rome, *Il Messaggero*.[39] The statement announced that American volunteers serving in the Finnish forces then fighting Russia would not lose their citizenship. On the same day, Warren read the report of the death of the chicken heart that scientist Alexis Carrel had kept alive in his laboratory. In an explanation of his use of the image of Carrel's chicken heart, kept "Alive in a test tube, where it monstrously grew, and slept," Warren reveals why this experiment struck him so forcefully:

---

39. Kimon Friar and John Malcolm Brinnin, eds., *Modern Poetry: British and American* (New York: Appleton-Century Crofts, 1951), 292–93. All subsequent references to this work will be noted parenthetically by page number.

The business about the chicken heart seemed to summarize a view current in our time—that science (as popularly conceived) will solve the problem of evil by reducing it merely to a matter of "adjustment" in the physical, social, economic, and political spheres. That same day I recalled a remark made in some book by John Strachey that after science had brought "adjustment" to society it would then solve the problem of evil by bringing man a mortal immortality, by abolishing disease and death. It struck me as somewhat strange that Strachey should equate physical death and evil on a point-to-point basis, and should thereby imply that good and physical survival are identical (292).

Warren then comments on his poem's indictment of the two views, stating that "for the purpose of the poem at least, I take a large component of that impulse to be the passionate emptiness and tidal lust of the modern man who, because he cannot find long-range meaning, seeks meaning in mere violence, the violence being what he wants and needs without reference ultimately to the political or other justification he may appeal to" (293). "Terror" thus levels serious charges against a society that believes itself free from the burdens of individual evil. Like the self-absorbed lovers in "Bearded Oaks" and "Picnic Remembered," the "you" of this poem stands accused of believing that "history is thus undone," wars and strife being simply events that happen elsewhere to other people. Even those who fight do so without purpose, "for their obsession knows / Only the immaculate itch, not human friends or foes" (*CP,* 78). War offers only a form of moral masturbation, like "The crime of Onan, spilled upon the ground," a sense of detached self-righteousness for the uninvolved who listen "by radio."

Nor can the problem of evil be rationalized through science. Carrel's experiment symbolized for Warren the tendency to reduce human significance to mere survival, transcendence being only a matter of prolonging physical existence. More than a century earlier, the Romantics had expressed similar misgivings over the prevailing notion held by Utilitarian philosophers that science could replace the mystery of human experience. Such "cold philosophy," Keats wrote in *Lamia,* "will empty the haunted air" and "unweave the rainbow," and Wordsworth warned of the "growing alienation and self-sufficiency of the understanding" as a result of scientific analysis and explanation.[40] From a scientific viewpoint, the heights and depths of human emotions—joy, passion, despair, and evil—become matters of intellect rather than necessary parts of the mystery of human experience. A scene similar to Carrel's experiment occurs in *All the King's Men*, as Jack Burden observes a "prefrontal lobectomy" conducted by his friend Adam Stanton. Jack sarcastically asks Adam if the patient would be "converted and baptized" after the surgery, and Adam innocently replies, "He will be different. . . . He will be perfectly happy" (*AKM*, 316). To the man of science, such an "adjustment" replaces the necessity for mystery or belief. As "Terror" warns, the individual cannot escape his humanity through the evasions offered by scientific abstraction or the "passionate emptiness" of violence. Warren does not conclude the poem with the remoteness of bloodshed in faraway countries or the sensationalism of Carrel's experiment. Instead, the closing scene chillingly suggests the domesticity of evil: "But you crack nuts, while the conscience-stricken stare / Kisses the terror; for you see an empty chair" (*CP*, 78). Implicated by isolation and guilt, the "you" in this poem becomes as much a part of evil as the ones who seek meaning through violence or scientific rationalization.

Despite claims by critics such as John L. Stewart that Warren's "acute perceptiveness [is] marred by even sillier overwriting," *Eleven Poems* shows remarkable development from the poetry of Warren's undergraduate days and even from his first published collection.[41] No longer was Warren content or willing to conduct his explorations within the metrical confines or gentle ironies espoused by Ransom. Nor was he inclined toward either the abstract reticence of Eliot's early poetry or the religious intensity of his later poetry. Indications of Eliot's influence remained constant throughout Warren's career, but the way that Warren modified many of the key elements he had

40. John Keats, "Lamia," in *Selected Poems*, ed. John Barnard (New York: Penguin Books, 1988), 193; Wordsworth, *Selected Poems and Prefaces*, ed. Stillinger, 456.

41. Stewart, *The Burden of Time*, 484.

"learned" from Eliot shows the steady development of his maturing, independent poetic voice. Eliot moved toward an increasingly orthodox vision, and his conversion to Christianity and the Anglican Church affected the overall mood and tone of his poems, especially in *Choruses from "The Rock"* (1934) and *Four Quartets* (1935–1942). Warren, however, continued to seek a philosophy by which he might embrace the world while maintaining his critical eye, unfettered by the strictures of orthodox religion. The search was not easy (nor would Warren have said it was ever resolved). For nearly a decade, stretching from 1944 to 1953, Warren faced the most serious challenge of his poetic career, what he later called "the drought." During this period of spiritual and aesthetic crisis, Warren sought not only a form but also a vision that would enable him to write the type of poetry that combined his pragmatic view of humankind with his emerging sense of human possibility.

"The Ballad of Billie Potts," Warren's last published effort before the onset of his poetic drought, reveals the direction of his developing interests. As in his earlier poetry, Warren juxtaposes past and present and continues to confront the discovery of guilt, the attempt at flight, and the necessity of return. But from 1944 until 1953, he published no poetry and instead turned to fiction and criticism. The next chapter takes a detailed look at "The Ballad of Billie Potts" as well as *Brother to Dragons*, two works that foreshadow the powerful Romantic strains that appear in *Promises: Poems, 1954–1956*. Searching for meaning out of the past was nothing new for Warren, and his novels of this period present characters groping toward self-knowledge and a sense of value in the present. During his decade of poetic silence, Warren continued his search for a vision that would integrate his recognition of man's fallen state with his perpetual yearning for significance. Ultimately, the English Romantics rendered such a vision possible for Warren.

II

"The Ballad of Billie Potts" and *Brother to Dragons*

Warren's first two volumes of poetry received substantial praise from reviewers, but the appearance of "The Ballad of Billie Potts," one of the three new poems in *Selected Poems, 1923–1943*, created the first real controversy over his work. In his 1944 review of "Billie Potts" in *Poetry*, Dudley Fitts applauded Warren's method of juxtaposing narrative with parenthesized asides, stating that "the concluding lines of the poem . . . meet in perfect resolution." F. W. Dupee, however, found the same method "weak and confused," and Horace Gregory concluded in his review of the poem that the structure presented "such violent lapses in taste that [he] became confused as to whether or not it was Jesse Stuart or Mr. Warren himself who dictated the lines." Even John Crowe Ransom, who in "The Inklings of 'Original Sin'" otherwise admired Warren's "clean-cut eloquence and technical accomplishments" in *Selected Poems, 1923–1943*, argued that the commentary was not "organically connected with the action of the plot," creating "a gloss . . . far more implausible than that which Coleridge wrote upon his margins."[1] Many of the critics who expressed discon-

1. Dudley Fitts, "Of Tragic Stature," review of *Selected Poems, 1923–1943*, by Robert Penn Warren, *Poetry* 65 (November 1944): 94–101; F. W. Dupee, "RPW and Others," review of *Selected Poems, 1923–1943*, by Robert Penn

tent with "Billie Potts" suggested that Warren's real skill lay in his shorter lyrics written in the Metaphysical vein, but Warren was on the verge of a critical breakthrough in his poetry, prepared to leave behind the techniques he had practiced since his Fugitive days at Vanderbilt. This breakthrough, however, was not to happen for nearly a decade. Although Warren's "poetic drought" troubled him from 1944 to 1953, during this period he was exploring other modes that would accommodate his emerging aesthetic. At this crucial point in his career, Warren's study of the English Romantics helped him to recover his poetic voice and to discover the voice that would later appear in some of his finest work.

"The Ballad of Billie Potts" was Warren's most inspired poetic effort of the 1940s, and it was the last poem he published before his dry spell. But it did not represent a dead end. Rather, as he told Peter Stitt in a 1977 interview, it was "a bridge piece, my jumping-off place when I started again, ten years later." In another 1977 interview, Warren explained that "Billie Potts" was a poem he "found something out by": "It's always been a kind of narrative streak in my poetry—or hints of narrative. It was primarily a philosophical poem—a poem about American history, philosophy of American history, and you can carry it further if you want to, theological—and then a ballad . . . I fused these two."[2] This fusion of ballad and introspective commentary was one of the most noticeable innovations of "Billie Potts," which blends colloquial ruralisms with the highly cerebral texture of

---

Warren, *Nation* 25 (November 1944): 660, 662; Horace Gregory, "Of Vitality, Regionalism, and Satire in Recent American Poetry," review of *Selected Poems, 1923–1943*, by Robert Penn Warren, *Sewanee Review* 52 (autumn 1944): 572–93; John Crowe Ransom, "The Inklings of 'Original Sin,'" review of *Selected Poems, 1923–1943*, by Robert Penn Warren, *Saturday Review* 20 (May 1944): 10–11. The "Jesse Stuart" that Gregory refers to in his review is the Kentucky farmboy/poet, known for his regional ballads.

  2. Robert Penn Warren, "An Interview with Robert Penn Warren," by Peter Stitt, in *Talking with Robert Penn Warren*, ed. Watkins et al., 239; Warren, "Reminiscences," interview by Farrell, *ibid.*, 296. The version of "The Ballad of Billie Potts" cited in this chapter is in *NSP*, 287–300.

many of his Fugitive poems. Although the ballad form may seem like an unlikely vehicle for complex philosophical exploration, Coleridge's *Rime* had shown Warren that the ballad structure could be used in precisely such a manner. As he wrote in "A Poem of Pure Imagination," "I see no reason to assume that a minor poetic form, in this case a ballad, would not be found worthy of serious development and serious freighting" (*SE*, 285). This defense of Coleridge's use of the ballad in turn reflects on Warren's own practice in "The Ballad of Billie Potts." Even as Warren was experimenting stylistically, he sustained his persistent evaluation of the human search for selfhood, confirming as he does in his earlier poetry the human need for self-knowledge.

Warren also takes a penetrating look at the delusion of human perfectibility, an issue he later developed as the central motif of *Brother to Dragons*. Unlike Emerson (at least as Warren interpreted him), Warren saw distinct problems with the belief that humans can transcend the most inward and primal impulses, evil in particular. He had addressed this issue in earlier poems, especially in "Terror," from *Eleven Poems on the Same Theme*. In an interview with Floyd Watkins in 1979, Warren explained that the discoveries he made while preparing for the essay on Coleridge corresponded with his own preoccupation with the idea of human perfectibility: "The first time I became aware of it as a central question for me was when I was writing the little book on Coleridge. Now Coleridge takes that view of perfectibility. I discovered it in 'The Ancient Mariner' itself—that this appeared in the poem. Preceding the book on 'The Ancient Mariner,' I had written a poem called 'Billie Potts,' which was my version of the same idea."[3] Though Warren asserts that his initial fascination with this topic was "not derived from Coleridge," he further says that "things exist in you without your knowing it." The fables presented in *Rime* and "The Ballad of Billie Potts," while original creations in themselves, recall stories as old as humankind. Warren's poem in par-

3. Robert Penn Warren, "A Dialogue with Robert Penn Warren on *Brother to Dragons*," interview by Floyd C. Watkins, in *Talking with Robert Penn Warren*, ed. Watkins et al., 342.

ticular reinforces the fundamental statement of "Original Sin: A Short Story": "Oh, nothing is lost, ever lost!" (*CP*, 69).

Developing many of the issues examined in Warren's earlier work, "Billie Potts" depicts the Fall of mankind, the loss of innocence, and the search for identity within a legend Warren had heard as a child. The folk ballad structure of the poem tells the story of a frontier family who ambushes and robs unsuspecting travelers, but the mythic parallels underlying the ballad transform Big Billie and his wife into a postlapsarian Adam and Eve, and Little Billie into the exiled and wandering Cain. While the literal setting of the poem is the area of Kentucky between the Cumberland and Tennessee Rivers, also known as "Between the Rivers," the repeated references to "the land between the rivers" link the Kentucky landscape with Mesopotamia, the original "land between the rivers" and theoretical site of the Garden of Eden. Yet this garden has already fallen, and its inhabitants are thieves and murderers. Part of what Warren sees as the fallacy of perfectibility is man's assumption that he can recover a primal innocence that does not exist—or, if it does, that is beyond the scope of human vision: "There was a beginning but you cannot see it" (*CP*, 82). The evil that Big Billie and his wife embody is a part of the human condition.

Combining folk ballad with introspective narrative commentary, Warren unfolds what Justus calls an "archetypal story of crime and punishment."[4] The device of the interpolated glosses, which Ransom found so implausible, connects the figures from regional legend with the general "you" that Warren addresses in earlier poems such as "Terror" and "Pursuit." The folksy cadences and dialect of the poem's narrative portions tell the story of Little Billie Potts, "A clabber-headed bastard with snot in his nose / And big red wrists hanging out of his clothes" (*CP*, 81), who must flee westward to escape being hanged after a blundered attempt to rob and murder a passing stranger. Yet throughout the poem, set aside parenthetically, Warren extends the scope of the poem to include "you," the collective body

4. Justus, *Achievement*, 17.

of humanity, both past and present. Even the modern "you," having committed no particular crimes, must also face the same passage that Little Billie experiences. Like the speaker in "Original Sin" who realizes that "Nothing is lost, ever lost," Little Billie's flight from fate only comes full circle in the end:

> There is always another country and always another place.
> There is always another name and another face.
> And the name and the face are you, and you
> The name and the face. . . .
>
> (*CP*, 85)

The search for self was a constant theme throughout Warren's earliest poetry, where he explored the various ways people try to suspend or avoid the progress of time and fate. However, as the voice in "Billie Potts" as well as the struggles of the protagonists in Warren's novels remind us, any efforts to escape our fates, or ourselves, is ultimately futile.

Although Ransom's comments on the "glosses" in "Billie Potts" were intended as criticism of Warren's experimentation, the connections between "Billie Potts" and *Rime of the Ancient Mariner* provide an important indication of the direction that Warren's poetry would take after he emerged from his "drought." Coleridge had long been a favorite of his (in *Portrait of a Father*, Warren describes his father reading the poem as one of his earliest and fondest memories), and Warren's study of Coleridge had begun during his New Critical work with Cleanth Brooks. Just prior to the publication of *Selected Poems, 1923–1943*, Warren had begun to prepare the essay on *Rime*, an analysis that not only interpreted the Romantic poem in New Critical fashion but also presented his perspective on such other Romantic poets as Blake, Wordsworth, Byron, Shelley, and Keats. Unlike Eliot, the younger poet found much in the Romantics that was praiseworthy and useful. In many ways, "A Poem of Pure Imagination" stands as a pivotal work that defines and anticipates the larger interests of his later works. His discussion of Coleridge's poem, insightful in itself, also offers a statement of Warren's own evolving poetic principles.

"The fable," Warren writes of the *Rime*, "is a story of crime and punishment and repentance and reconciliation" (*SE*, 222). This phrase could be applied equally to "The Ballad of Billie Potts," and the similarities between it and Coleridge's poem are both thematic and structural. In addition to the controversial "glosses," the figure of the Mariner serves as an antecedent to Little Billie Potts. Because of their crimes, both men become exiles, propelled by violence into separation and loss. Little Billie thus joins the Mariner in a long literary tradition of exiles whose behavior is characterized by Harold Bloom as "a desperate assertion of self and a craving for a heightened sense of identity."[5] Both Coleridge's Mariner and Warren's frontier outlaw are defined by the acts they commit, and both, however painfully or unwillingly, must face the consequences of their actions.

These broad and rather general similarities may appear less significant once we consider the different outcomes of each poem. The Mariner, after his initial crime and its punishment, finally rejoins what Warren calls the "sacramental vision of the universe" by blessing the sea snakes. The albatross falls from his neck, allowing him to begin the long journey home, but his penance continues in his eternal ritual of storytelling. In "A Poem of Pure Imagination," Warren writes, "In the end [the Mariner] accepts the sacramental view of the universe, and his will is released from its state of 'utmost abstraction' and gains the state of 'immanence' in wisdom and love" (*SE*, 233). In "The Ballad of Billie Potts," however, Little Billie is denied the penitential purging that the Mariner undergoes. Big Billie and his wife fail to recognize their son when he returns to his family home, nor does Little Billie disclose his identity. Mistaking their prodigal son for another wealthy traveler, the Potts murder, rob, and bury Little Billie "in the dark of the trees" (*CP*, 89). Yet there is a reconciliation, even in death. The correspondent aside recapitulates the impetus of Little Billie's return as well as his destruction:

5. Harold Bloom, *The Visionary Company: A Reading of English Romantic Poetry* (Ithaca: Cornell University Press, 1971), 202.

So, weary of greetings now and the new friend's smile,
Weary in art of the stranger, worn with your wanderer's wile,
Weary of innocence and the husks of Time,
You come, back to the homeland of no-Time,
To ask forgiveness and the patrimony of your crime;
And kneel in the untutored night as to demand
What gift—oh, father, father—from that dissevering hand?

(*CP*, 89)

After his long exile, the son returns home and bows his head to his father, who is "ignorant and evil and old," signifying Little Billie's as well as his parents' penance, for they, too, are complicit.

Little Billie's death releases him from his exile and his fate, but his story—the narrative itself—is not the final word in the poem. The ballad ends by including the "you" in the poem within the scope of Little Billie's sacrifice. Thus we, the readers, become the ones who are left to tell our own stories, to seek our fates in "The itch and humble promise" (*CP*, 91) of lost innocence. The glosses remind us that the archetypal journey unfolded through the story of Little Billie is more than an allegory. As Warren noted, the fable of the Mariner is "not merely a device for creating an illusion" (*SE*, 203). Similarly, Warren's poem is not merely a folk fable. Justus finds that the glosses, although more stylistically complex than the ballad portions, bring the poem into organic unity: "The effect of the high style is not simply to generalize from a specific historical-legendary story but to turn that generalization back into application that is immediate and even more intimately specific than the narrative itself: these segments are really asides to 'you.'"[6] These "asides" draw the reader into the past, into the story of Little Billie with all its implications of guilt and complicity. Warren finds the same relevance in Coleridge's poem, arguing that "we must remember that in so far as the poem is truly the poet's, in so far as it ultimately expresses him, it involves his own view of the world, his own values. Therefore the poem will, for better or

6. Justus, *Achievement*, 58.

worse, have relevance, by implication at least, to the world outside the poem" (*SE*, 303). In "The Ballad of Billie Potts," we become the "mariners" who must evaluate the losses and gains of our experience and live out the story of flight, return, and reconciliation repeatedly. The "you" of the poem is then the wanderer, seeking to find that illusory unity, trying to discover some sort of truth by which to live.

Part of the lesson that the "you" of the poem must learn, in the midst of modern disillusionment, resembles the reconstitution into the "One Life" that Warren sees as the central integrative motif of Coleridge's poem. Finding no meaning in the past, the "you" in the poem has no sense of wholeness or identity "At the hour when the ways are darkened." Modern man may not have any literal albatrosses to bear or sea snakes to bless, but on a symbolic level, as Warren points out, "the imagination in its value-creating capacity" transforms familiar elements of experience into symbolic indicators of deeper meaning (*SE*, 236). In Warren's poem, reminders from the past signify the same dark impulses that the Mariner must reconcile himself to in order to receive partial absolution. Warren places this vision of the past within the context of familiar scenes, captured "Rapt in the fabulous complacency of fresco, vase, or frieze":

> The answer is in the back of the book but the page is gone.
> And Grandma told you to tell the truth, but she is dead.
> And heedless, their hairy faces fixed
> Beyond your call or question now, they move
> Under the fatuate weight of their wisdom,
> Precious but for the preciousness of their burden.
>
> (*CP*, 83)

Like the speaker in "Original Sin," the "you" in "Billie Potts" tries to escape the "burden" of the past, seeking "A sense of cleansing and hope which blooms from distress." But flight proves illusory, even though

> in the new country and in the new place
> The eyes of the new friend will reflect the new face

And his mouth will speak to frame
The syllables of the new name.

(*CP*, 86)

Reminiscent of Jack Burden's westward journey in *All the King's Men*, the poet depicts the allure of escape: "For Time is motion / For Time is innocence / For Time is West" (*CP*, 86).

Yet, as Jack Burden of *All the King's Men*, Jeremiah Beaumont of *World Enough and Time*, and other protagonists in Warren's poetry and fiction discover, the assumption that one can undo the past proves delusive and even dangerous. In earlier poems, such as "The Return: An Elegy" and "Kentucky Mountain Farm," speakers similarly seek to regain the lost innocence of childhood and home, only to find "all / Familiar faithless things would yet remain / Voiceless" (*CP*, 38). In this sense, Warren echoes the Romantic problem of reconciling the illusion of the past self with the diminished vision of the present self. For the "you" in "Billie Potts," the facile assurances of daily life may engender a certain superficial satisfaction, but any inward source of self-knowledge is prevented by a lack of awareness taken from the continuity of experience. Although "you" may become wealthy or admired, "Though your conscience was easy and you were assured of your innocence" (*CP*, 88) "you" gradually become aware that "something was missing from the picture": "'Why, I'm not in it at all!'" Thus, like Little Billie, "you decided to retrace your steps from that point," back home, on a mission to find "whatever it was you had lost" (*CP*, 88).

Yet like the terrible "treasure" that the mad killer in "Crime" has "buried under the leaves," whatever incriminating elements of self that that have been buried will eventually resurface. As Charles H. Bohner notes in his discussion of "Billie Potts," the past and the self are indivisible, "even though in seeking the source of his life he [Little Billie and modern man] may, ironically, find death."[7] Warren em-

---

7. Charles H. Bohner, *Robert Penn Warren* (New York: Twayne, 1964), 59.

phasizes how "you," Narcissus-like, gaze into the stream not "to drink of the stream but of your deep identity" (*CP*, 85), but "the reflection is shadowy and the form not clear" (*CP*, 89). Although this passage may seem to imply the indifference of time and nature, the images suggest that bound up within time is "the pool" of the individual self:

> But perhaps what you lost was lost in the pool long ago
> When childlike you lost it and then in your innocence rose to go
> After kneeling, as now, with your thirst beneath the leaves.
>
> (*CP*, 89)

This implacable "thirst" for renewal and self-knowledge compels the individual to engage in this return, although whatever has been left behind, as Warren hints, "lies here and dreams in the depths and grieves" (*CP*, 89).

So why does Little Billie come home, under shade of twilight in disguise, for a reunion with his murderous parents? And why does the "you" in this poem commit the symbolic equivalent of returning to the past? Jack Burden finds that "the end of man is knowledge" (*AKM*, 9) as well as the justification for his being, and this concern emerges as the primary motif in "The Ballad of Billie Potts." The struggle toward self-knowledge involves the recognition of one's connection to a fallen world and an acceptance of the corruption within the self. In a passage that foreshadows the dominant image of man's bestiality in *Brother to Dragons*, Warren correlates the human compulsion for return ("the itch and humble promise which is home") (*CP*, 91) with the animal instinct for migration. The bee, the eel, and the goose instinctively know the necessity of the "long return," and the "salmon heaves at the fall." But the "wanderer, you," apart from reason, must "Heave at the great fall of Time" (*CP*, 91):

> And you, wanderer, back,
> Brother to pinion and the pious fin that cleave
> The innocence of air and the disinfectant flood
> And wing and welter and weave

The long compulsion and the circuit hope
Back

(*CP*, 91)

Like Warren's version of Thomas Jefferson, "you" are "brother to pinion," "brother to dragons and a companion to owls" (Job 30:29). Although acknowledging this relationship does "murder" the past self, it also offers the chance to participate in a more fully realized humanity, Coleridge's "One Life." In Warren's reading of the *Rime*, the Mariner, who initially rejects any kinship with the "slimy creatures of the deep," later recognizes their beauty and begins the long process toward redemption. His penance never ends, but he is at least able to walk among a "goodly company," heavy with the burden of contrition and blessedness.[8] In "Billie Potts," the prodigal "you"— every human being, the poet himself included—kneels "in the sacramental silence of evening / At the feet of the old man / Who is evil and ignorant and old" (*CP*, 92) to accept the stroke of identity, complicity, and knowledge.

With the publication of *Brother to Dragons: A Tale in Verse and Voices* in 1953, Warren's ten-year poetic drought was broken, and his poetry from *Promises: Poems 1954–1956* forward offers a glimpse at possibilities previously absent from his work: the capacity for reconciliation and joy. Warren's new marriage and the subsequent births of his children had altered his personal outlook dramatically, and his Romantic "conversion" of the mid-1940s enabled him to infuse his poetry with a growing sense of hopefulness. Warren had been working on *Brother to Dragons* during his drought, utilizing the dramatic and narrative structures that he had been exploring in earlier works such as "The Ballad of Billie Potts" and *Proud Flesh*, the play version of *All the King's Men*. Writing fiction also helped him clarify ideas that later appear in his poetry. Warren commented in an interview following the publication of *Brother to Dragons* that "the poetry has

8. Coleridge, *The Rime of the Ancient Mariner*, in *Samuel Taylor Coleridge*, ed. Jackson, 54, 64.

gone along with the fiction," resulting in a kind of hybrid": "[*Brother to Dragons*] even started out to be a novel, and though it is in verse and is a poem, it has a complicated narrative and involves many fictional problems." Although the shorter lyric structures that had been the mainstay of Warren's early career appear less frequently in his later poetry, *Promises* demonstrates his ability to create sequences of shorter poems while developing the personalized voice of his later poems. Both *Brother to Dragons* and *Promises*, however different they may appear in structure, subject, and tone, submit a vision of the world that, in the final analysis, is much the same vision that the Romantics held: that the world is "all of one piece," and that, as Karl Kroeber has claimed in his study of the Romantics, "good and evil, innocence and experience, sensual passion and spiritual passion are definite, irreducible components out of whose interactions the processes of human experience arise."[9]

On the surface, *Brother to Dragons* may appear antithetical to Romanticism. The "tale in verse and voices" presents the most extreme forms of human depravity, and the focal act of violence is the brutal murder of a young slave named George, by Thomas Jefferson's nephews, Lilburn and Isham Lewis. Many critics maintain that the poem is an attack on Romanticism, but quite often their definition of Romanticism translates into a generic notion of idealism. One could speculate that such a misinterpretation of Romantic theory evolved in part from the New Critical bias against the Romantics, chiefly led by Eliot's own attacks against the "immaturity" of Romantic poetry. But the Romantics were not exempt from their own explorations of the darker side of human nature—they did not write poems simply about flowers and birds and idiot children. As M. H. Abrams writes in *Natural Supernaturalism*, "The subjects of Wordsworth's narrative poems are man's inhumanity to man, gross social injustice, destitute and helpless old age, guilt and sorrow, seduction and abandonment, infanticide, the steady deterioration of character under the pressure

9. Warren, "A Self-Interview," in *Talking with Robert Penn Warren*, ed. Watkins et al., 2; Karl Kroeber, *Romantic Narrative Art* (Madison: University of Wisconsin Press, 1960), 69.

of unmerited and immitigable suffering, the fortitude of men who possess no other recourse against bitter circumstance, [and] the sudden loss of a beloved child." Abrams further asserts that "a critic's charge that Romantic writers neglected the problem of evil is probably only a way of saying that he does not approve of their solution to the problem."[10]

The problem of evil figures as the most primary and urgent issue in *Brother to Dragons*. The dramatic circumstance of the poem involves an actual historical event, although in his foreword Warren admits to taking significant poetic liberties: "I am trying to write a poem and not a history, and therefore have no compunction about tampering with the facts" (*BD*, [1953], xii).[11] For the purpose of his poem, Warren presents an array of speakers meeting in "no time and no place." Ghostly voices converse with the poet and with each other, relating their accounts of the past. Warren enters the poem in the persona of "R.P.W.," and the personalized voice of the poet as narrator acts as a guiding consciousness for the other speakers. He takes the historical account of a young slave's brutal murder at the hands of Jefferson's nephews and transforms it into an exploration of the tensions between idealism and realism, self and other, separation and reconciliation.

The Thomas Jefferson that Warren introduces in the poem is in many ways the historical personage revered in the annals of American greatness. Described in the dramatis personae as "the third President

10. M. H. Abrams, *Natural Supernaturalism: Tradition and Revolution in Romantic Literature* (New York: Norton, 1971), 443.

11. For the purposes of my discussion at this point, I will be citing the 1953 edition of *Brother to Dragons*. Warren himself preferred his 1979 version of the poem, and his foreword to this later edition notes his "dissatisfaction with several features" of the 1953 poem. In his discussion of *Brother to Dragons* in *Robert Penn Warren and the American Imagination* (Athens: University of Georgia Press, 1990), Hugh Ruppersburg also chooses the 1979 version, stating that that poem is "more dramatic, less didactic, and less polemical than the original" (42). Out of chronological considerations, however, here I refer to the 1953 version.

of the United States, who bought the Great West from Napoleon" and (in reference to the inscription on his tombstone) "Author of the Declaration of Independence [,] Of The Statute of Virginia For Religious Freedom, And Father of the University of Virginia" (*BD* [1953], 2), the Jefferson of history provides the contextual referent of the poem. But it is not Jefferson's "triple boast," at least not directly, that Warren concerns himself with in his vision (or re-vision) of history. Rather, as Hugh Ruppersburg points out, "The central conflict of this poem develops out of the apparent fact that Jefferson never in his lifetime mentioned his nephew's murder" of a slave.[12] Warren takes this omission, enlarges it by placing the crimes of the past alongside the turmoil of American history, and offers it to Jefferson with all its implications of bloody complicity. Thus, the crux of the poem develops into Warren's imagined encounter between Lilburn Lewis and Jefferson. Initially, Jefferson resists the notion of his own inherent connection with evil, but in the course of the poem he comes to realize his place in the "One Life," through the necessary recognition of his own moral culpability.

Like any good adherent of the Enlightenment, Jefferson in *Brother to Dragons* reacts with shock and dismay as he confronts the evil of his nephews' act. In acknowledging this evil, he must not only admit the error of his notion of human perfectibility but also recognize the mixture of good and evil in all humans, including himself. The title of the poem comes from Job 30:29 ("I am a brother to dragons and a companion to owls"). Strandberg comments on the significance of the biblical allusion, explaining that "Warren's attention is focused not on Job's suffering and loss and endurance, but upon the one thing [Jefferson] could not endure—his loss of pride."[13] The "pride" that Jefferson holds is in his "identity with the definition of man" (*BD* [1953], 127), but as R.P.W. later argues, such a reckoning must eventually find a "new definition":

> "If I had known—" and once you say those words
> You'll end by saying all those other words

12. Ruppersburg, *American Imagination*, 39.
13. Strandberg, *Poetic Vision*, 170–71.

You've said, and the great Machine of History
Will mesh its gears sweetly in that sweet lubrication
Of human regret, and the irreversible
Dialectic will proceed. That is, unless—
"If I had known"—that is, unless we get
Some new and better definition of *knowing*.

(*BD* [1953], 127)

In the nightmare world of *Brother to Dragons*, knowledge is achieved only at a painful cost. R.P.W. rebukes Jefferson for his idealized vision of humankind but does not permit him to sink into the opposite extreme of naturalistic despair. Neither excessive optimism nor bleak pessimism takes into account the irremediable fusion of good and evil. Accepting this knowledge of self requires constant and often agonizing examination, for as Jack Burden realizes, "the end of man is to know" (*AKM*, 9).

The desire to "know" motivates Warren's tormented speakers in almost all of his early poetry, but they are often propelled only into further confusion and a sense of loss chiefly because of the knowledge they gain. However, in Warren's reading of Coleridge's *Rime*, confusion and loss are converted into possibilities for redemption, the opportunity to participate in the "One Life." This is not to say that the past has been eradicated; the event that sets the Mariner's suffering in motion is in the past, but he must repeat his tale, again and again, to achieve his own penance as well as to instruct others of the lesson he has learned. Confronting the past burdens both Mariner figures in *Brother to Dragons*, and as a product of the poet's imagination, Jefferson is "summoned" to face the self that *was* and the nation—which he see as a timeless extension of himself—that *is*. Structurally, *Brother to Dragons* offers a more sophisticated use of the interpolated glosses that Warren had utilized in "The Ballad of Billie Potts." Thematically, the poem dramatizes Warren's fascination with Coleridge's philosophy of poetry, life, and the imagination as well as his fable of the wandering Mariner.

As Justus, Randy Hendricks, and other Warren scholars have pointed out, Warren's version of the Mariner figure recurs throughout his work. Justus argues that Warren's use of Coleridge's patterns assumes both moral and aesthetic forms: "The burden of man's salvation requires adequate verbalization . . . [and] that verbalizing assumes formal, appropriate, even ritualistic shapes."[14] Percy Munn of *Night Rider*, Jerry Calhoun of *At Heaven's Gate*, and Jeremiah Beaumont of *World Enough and Time* (all written before *Brother to Dragons*) encounter Mariner figures (Ashby Wyndham and Willie Proudfit, for example) who tell stories of sin and redemption. Though we as readers may realize the import of these moral lessons, Warren's protagonists often fail to understand what Jack Burden eventually comprehends, that "the world is all of one piece" (*AKM*, 188), and that any action, regardless of intention, has immeasurable consequences for both the self and others.

Significantly, in *All the King's Men* (the novel interrupted by Warren's study of Coleridge), Jack Burden does attain the vision of moral acceptance denied to Warren's other protagonists. As Ruppersburg observes, "Of Warren's fictional protagonists, Jefferson most resembles Jack Burden."[15] Like Burden, Jefferson moves from humanistic idealism to shocked despair following his realization that a member of his own family—his own blood—has committed an atrocity. We know from Warren's depiction of Burden that no critic is harsher than the disillusioned idealist. In his more cynical moods, Burden refers to his past self as a "brass-bound idealist"; likewise, Jefferson reacts in horror and bewilderment as the reality of evil overshadows his glorious vision of humankind. In *All the King's Men*, the reader becomes the "Wedding Guest" to Burden's story, but in *Brother to Dragons*, the poet himself, as R.P.W., plays that role, serving as a foil to both Jefferson's exalted conception of humanity and his subsequent despondency.

14. See section II ("Mariners") of chapter 1 in Justus's *Achievement*, which is an excellent study of Warren's body of work, as well as Randy J. Hendricks's insightful discussion of Warren's Mariner figures ("Warren's Wandering Son," *South Atlantic Review* 59, no. 2 [May 1994]: 75–93). The passage from Justus cited in the text appears on page 25 of his book.

15. Ruppersburg, *American Imagination*, 45.

For the Mariner's message to be effective, it must also alter the moral understanding of the recipient, and R.P.W. stands to learn much the same lesson that Jefferson must realize. When Jefferson comments on R.P.W.'s overt cynicism—"What I lack, my friend, is the absolute dream and joy / That I once had, and that from the way you talk / I doubt you ever had . . ."—R.P.W. sardonically admits that the "absolute dream and joy" "is scarcely / The most fashionable delusion of my age, and I—/ I simply never had it" (*BD* [1953], 48). R.P.W.'s sentiments here sound remarkably like the voice heard in Warren's early poems, especially the voice that remarks to his dead mother in "The Return: An Elegy" that "if you possessed conveniently enough three eyes / then I could buy a pack of cigarettes" (*CP*, 33).

Although the figure of R.P.W. is, for the most part, a version of the poet, it is not safe to assume that Warren advocated the nihilism of R.P.W.'s stance at the beginning of the poem.[16] More plausibly, since Warren identifies R.P.W. as "the writer of this poem" in the dramatis personae, R.P.W. could also be seen as a projection of Warren's crisis as a poet. R.P.W. comments at one point that finding the form for his poem was just as daunting as the problem of self-discovery:

> No, the action is not self-contained, but contains
> Us too, and is contained by us, and is
> Only an image of the issue of our most distressful self-definition.
> And so to put the story in a ballad
> Would be like shoveling a peck of red-hot coals
> In a crocker sack to tote them down the road
> To start the fire in a neighbor's fireplace.
> You won't get far with them, even if you run—
> No, the form was not adequate to the material.
>
> (*BD* [1953], 43–44)

16. Ruppersburg reaches a similar conclusion on this point, stating that R.P.W.'s cynicism "marks a modern way of thinking that Warren finds dan-

Thus, *Brother to Dragons* is ultimately not just a poem about Thomas Jefferson. It is a poem about Warren as well, just as his later work, *Audubon: A Vision*, combines the poetic vision of the historical ornithologist's search for meaning with the poet's personal explorations of selfhood. R.P.W. is not a priest who hears Jefferson's confession, nor is he merely "a commentator on the action."[17] Unlike Jefferson, R.P.W. appears resigned to the notion of evil. His lesson, therefore, is to make a "new acquaintance with the nature of joy" (*BD* [1953], 209).

This "new acquaintance with the nature of joy" signals the progress that both R.P.W. and Jefferson make from their initial delusions about human nature toward their hard-earned conceptions of the possibility of human virtue. The presence of R.P.W.'s father, much like Wordsworth's leech gatherer in "Resolution and Independence," offers the poet a glimpse of "human strength, by apt admonishment"[18] or, in the context of Warren's poem, the "bitter percoon" of knowledge and experience. Paralleling R.P.W.'s metaphorical taking of his father's hand in recognition of the past and the joy that can arise out of living, Jefferson's sister Lucy, mother of Lilburn and Isham, encourages her brother to take Lilburn's hand:

> If you would assume the burden of innocence—and dear Brother,
> I must say to you now, for it comes now strangely to me to say it,
> That the burden of innocence is heavier than the burden of guilt—
> But what I mean to say, if you would assume the burden of innocence
> . . . you must take
> His hand—
>
> (*BD* [1953], 191)

---

gerous and reprehensible. . . . Warren surely did not advocate these attitudes. Nor should he advocate them in a persona with his initials" (*ibid.*, 71).

17. Frederick P. W. McDowell, "Psychology and Theme in *Brother to Dragons*," *PMLA* 70 (September 1955): 572.

18. Wordsworth, "Resolution and Independence," in *Selected Poems and Prefaces*, ed. Stillinger, 169.

Although Jefferson initially recoils ("To take it, and the blood slick on it?"), he finds it within himself to admit his moral complicity and human frailty. In his final appearance in the poem, Jefferson offers his prayer of blessing:

> Dance back the buffalo, the shining land!
> Our grander Ghost Dance dance now, and shake the feather.
> Dance back the morning and the eagle's cry.
> Dance back the Shining Mountains, let them shine!
>
> (*BD* [1953], 195)

Although the tone of this blessing comes across as rather forced and desperate, the concluding lines resound with the power that Warren had earlier asserted in "Original Sin" ("Oh, nothing is lost, ever lost! at last you understood") (*CP*, 69).

> For nothing we had,
> Nothing we were,
> Is lost.
> All is redeemed,
> In knowledge.
> But knowledge is the most powerful cost . . .
> In joy, I would end.
>
> (*BD* [1953], 194)

Near the end of the poem, Jefferson, in Warren's imagination, can now return to his final rest, but R.P.W. must continue to "walk in the world" and carry with him the burden of his knowledge. When Jefferson says, "We are condemned to some hope," R.P.W. becomes the living purveyor of that hope, and he has the last word in the poem. As both Wedding Guest and Mariner, R.P.W. must figuratively bless his own "foul sea-snakes" (most dramatically imagined in the poem as the mud-slimed catfish who is "One with God" and the snake, "fat old *obsoleta*, who rears its head in "the paralyzed light") (*BD* [1953], 33) both internal and external. Conscious of the burden

of his "new acquaintance with the nature of joy," R.P.W. considers
the isolation of knowledge, the awareness of love and separateness:

> I have been a stranger at the breaking of bread.
> I have been a stranger at the monstrous conversation of ocean,
> And when the pretty child laid a hand on my knee.
> I have, in other words, shared the most common
> Human experience, which makes all mankind one,
> For isolation is the common lot,
> And paradoxically, it is only by
> That isolation that we know how to name
> The human bond and thus define the self.
>
> (*BD* [1953], 205–206)

Like the Ancient Mariner, Warren begins his return journey with a
literal blessing. As he looks upon the Ohio River, he realizes the final
redemptive vision of the men who have lived and died before him:
"And I thought how men had moved on that broad flood, / The
good, the bad, the strong, the weak . . ." (*BD* [1953], 209). He returns
to the car where his father waits for him, entering "a world / Sweeter
than hope in that confirmation of late light" (*BD* [1953], 215).

Brother to Dragons is on the whole a poem about America, both
past and present, and Warren's lifelong commitment to examining
the paradoxes of its history and myths. Yet the concluding vision of
this poem (as unsatisfying as many critics find it) is one of Romantic
reconciliation. Jefferson, like the Mariner, must find meaning in the
deepest, most despised elements he discovers within and without
himself; his "slimy things of the deep" are the bestial inclinations that
lurk beneath his surface of enlightened humanism. R.P.W., on the
other hand, recognizes the darker aspects of the human psyche but
must come to terms with the notion of the nobility, even the glory,
inherent in the seemingly futile strivings of humankind: "But still,
despite all naturalistic considerations, / Or in the end because of naturalistic considerations, / We must believe in virtue" (*BD* [1953], 29).
Each man's progress toward an individual conception of Coleridge's
"One Life" follows the Romantic precept of the reconciliation of op-

posites, for as R.P.W. learns from the lessons of history and from his own inner delvings into the self, "The recognition of complicity is the beginning of innocence" (*BD* [1953], 214).

What becomes most evident in *Brother to Dragons* and the other poems following Warren's Romantic "conversion" is his increasing emphasis on the possibility of joy "despite naturalistic considerations" (*BD* [1953], 29). The "joy" that Warren's speakers yearn for is the same joy that M. H. Abrams defines in Romantic terms as "the attempt to recover in maturity an earlier stage of integrity with oneself and the outer world, in a mode of consciousness for which the standard name is 'joy.'" In preparing to write "A Poem of Pure Imagination," Warren was involved not only in the process of examining Coleridge's famous ballad (following the patterns of New Critical analysis) but also of understanding the philosophy that shaped and guided the Romantic imagination. "Joy" is a central and recurrent term in the Romantic vocabulary, and like the Romantics, Warren invests the term with specialized meaning. In Coleridge's philosophy of the one and the many, "joy" signifies "the conscious accompaniment of the activity of a fully living and integrative mind." As Abrams further explains, "'hope' and 'joy,' as against 'despair' and 'dejection,' was a central and recurrent antithesis in Romantic poetry."[19] At the time that *Brother to Dragons* was written, Warren seemed reluctant to affirm a complete notion of joy, describing it as "the keen / Appetitive spur and that delicious delusion" (*BD* [1953], 209). Only later in his career could he proclaim, "Delusion?—No! For Truth has many moments" (*CP*, 581).

In *Brother to Dragons*, R.P.W. realizes that, along with the suffering that knowledge entails, comes not only joy but innocence, a "new definition" of innocence not circumscribed by prelapsarian unconsciousness or regression. We have seen in Warren's earlier poetry the futility of "backward flight," especially in "The Return: An Elegy," where the speaker wishes for a return to childhood to escape the pain of mature awareness. In *Brother to Dragons*, however, R.P.W. insists

---

19. Abrams, *Natural Supernaturalism*, 123, 276, 329.

upon the incorporation of memory and imagination into the fullness of being:

> . . . oh, I remember
> That much from the old times when like any boy
> I thought to name the world and hug it tight,
> And snake and hawk and fox and ant and day and night
> All moved in a stately pavane of great joy
> And naked danced before the untouchable Ark of Covenant,
> Like Israel's king, and never one fell down.
>
> (*BD* [1953], 34–35)

Warren, like Wordsworth, recalls the power of childhood vision, the "glad animal movements" that imbue the child with a perception denied to the mature eye, but neither Wordsworth's nor Warren's use of memory implies the celebration of that childhood vision at the expense of the knowledge gained in maturity.

In "Tintern Abbey," Wordsworth describes the "dizzy raptures" of boyhood, but his experienced faculties discern that "that time is past, / And all its aching joys are now no more." Yet, such a loss does not necessarily constitute a dirge for irretrievable youth, for "other gifts / Have followed; for such a loss, I would believe, abundant recompense." Part of that "recompense" includes an awareness of "The still, sad music of humanity," a sound that R.P.W. appears all too willing to succumb to at first, but the knowledge that age brings also introduces "the joy / Of elevated thoughts" and "a sense sublime / Of something far more deeply interfused."[20] In a passage reflective of Wordsworth's "Tintern Abbey," R.P.W. offers the same chastening perspective of memory: "But when you're not a boy you learn one thing: / You settle for what you get. You find that out" (*BD* [1953], 35). But Warren (or R.P.W.), also like Wordsworth, concludes that the vision earned is a vital part of living, because if one "settles" for

20. Wordsworth, "Lines Composed a Few Miles above Tintern Abbey," in *Selected Poems and Prefaces*, ed. Stillinger, 110.

the notion of the self divorced from the world and nature, "you're good as dead."

Warren was not even content to "settle" for his first version of *Brother to Dragons*. A quarter century later, he published a new version and referred to it as a "new work" (*BD*, xiii). Harold Bloom, uneasy with the 1953 version's "ideological tendentiousness," reviewed the 1979 poem generously, expressing admiration for Warren's "revisionary skill and intellectual persistence."[21] A few comments on the 1979 version are necessary here in light of Warren's Romantic evolution. Warren himself preferred the 1979 version over his earlier effort, and his insistence that the 1979 version provides a new dimension to his previous work signals his awareness of the shift in his aesthetic development. The two versions are thematically similar and the plot remains essentially unchanged, but the tone of the later poem is one of greater humility. Much of the self-righteousness disappears from R.P.W.'s exchanges with Jefferson, suggesting that in the twenty-five years between versions, Warren had achieved a level of compassion and personal acceptance beyond the accusatory stance assumed in the 1953 poem. My discussion of Warren's later poetry in Chapter 5 includes another look at the 1979 *Brother to Dragons* and how this version of the poem reflects the maturity of his Romantic vision. At this point, an exploration of the collection that follows the 1953 *Brother to Dragons* is not only due but imperative, for *Promises: Poems, 1954–1956* quietly announces Warren's most fully realized Romantic vision in the aftermath of his poetic dry spell.

Promises took many critics by surprise, accustomed as they were to the grim appraisal of humanity that permeates the earlier poetry. The poems in *Promises* present glimpses of joy and hope, but Warren does not abandon the darker impulses of naturalism that dominate his previous volumes. Evil exists in Warren's world and is very real, and the possibilities of redemption are often dimmed by what Jeremiah Beaumont in *World Enough and Time* calls "the moil and clutter of the

---

21. Harold Bloom, review of *Brother to Dragons* by Robert Penn Warren, *New Republic*, September 30, 1978, p. 34.

world" (*WET*, 459). Yet in *Promises*, Warren's yearning voice powerfully and poignantly affirms his belief in "Time's irremediable joy" (*CP*, 141) and "Truth's glare-glory" (*CP*, 126). For Warren, as for his Romantic ancestors, the power of the imagination yields this vision of possibility and hope.

III

Promises and Warren's Romantic Vision

In a 1957 interview with Ralph Ellison and Eugene Walter, Robert Penn Warren explained the change he experienced during the 1940s in his "personal relation" toward his writing: "I quit writing poems for several years. . . . I'd start them, get a lot down, then feel that I wasn't connecting somehow. I didn't finish one for several years, they felt false. Then I got back at it, and that is the bulk of what I've done since *Band of Angels*—a new book of poems."[1] This "new book of poems," *Promises*, was the first volume of lyric poetry Warren had published since *Selected Poems, 1923–1943* thirteen years earlier, and it won the Pulitzer Prize and National Book Award in 1958. As its title suggests, the collection presents a "dawning perspective and possibility of good" (*CP*, 126). Compared to *Brother to Dragons*, *Promises* exhibits what Morgan Blum calls "a more distinctive ability to find emblems of grace and redemption . . . amid conditions of filth and decay." John L. Stewart, who previously offered harsh criticism of the 1953 *Brother to Dragons*, extols the merits of *Promises*: "In scope, tragic sense, mastered substance, inventiveness, and plain power *Promises*

---

1. Quoted in Malcolm Cowley, *Writers at Work* (New York: Random House, 1959), 195.

surpasses all other volumes of verse published in this country since the Second World War."[2]

The capacity for joy and belief that emerges in *Promises* signals perhaps the most significant imaginative shift in Warren's career. If readers in 1957 were astounded by this seemingly new development in Warren's poetry, the tone of poems such as "The Flower" and "The Necessity for Belief" suggests his wonder at apprehending the possibility within himself. The theme of the "One Life" and the "sacramental vision" of the universe that Warren found central to the Romantic imagination emerges in his "post-drought" poetry as a forceful indicator of the influence that his immersion in Romantic poetry had on his poetic development. In *Brother to Dragons* and *Promises*, "The world is real. It is there," as Warren acknowledges in "Court-martial," but it is a world that can yield whatever meaning humans are able to obtain (*CP*, 113). The labyrinth of horror and fear, so powerfully rendered in both poetic works, is very much a part of the world Warren documents. But in *Promises*, the labyrinth opens into light, hope, and the possibility of "Time's irremediable joy" (*CP*, 141). These possibilities for joy, Wordsworth's "abundant recompense," lie at the heart of Warren's Romantic vision.

Warren himself frequently acknowledged the significance of *Promises* as a "breakthrough" in his career. In a 1977 interview with David Farrell, he clarified what the book signified for him: "*Promises* was discovery, starting all over again. From 1944 to '54 I must have started fifty poems, had gotten three or four or ten lines and threw them away, couldn't carry them through. One thing, I was tied up in fiction. One thing, I had, I guess, more personal problems than I should have had. . . . But in '54, suddenly a new place, a new time, a

---

2. Morgan Blum, "Promises as Fulfillment," *Kenyon Review* 21 (winter 1959): 97; Stewart, *The Burden of Time*, 515. Not all of the critical response to *Promises* was so favorable. Kenneth Koch, known for his scathing parodies of William Carlos Williams and Robert Frost, targeted Warren's poetry of this period for ridicule. In his poem "Fresh Air," Koch satirizes Warren's poem I of *Promises* (to Gabriel, "What Was the Promise That Smiled from the Maples at Evening?").

new life."[3] The "personal problems" included his unhappy marriage to Emma Brescia and his divorce in 1951.[4] His subsequent marriage to Eleanor Clark obviously made him a much happier man, and he told Marshall Walker in 1969 that "there was suddenly just this new sense of *release*—so the short poems began to come in that year [original emphasis]." The births of his children, Rosanna and Gabriel, also contributed to a "new outlook." Warren not only dedicated the volume to his children but also made them the primary subjects of the majority of the poems. Leonard Casper maintains in *Robert Penn Warren: The Dark and Bloody Ground* that "the poems [in *Promises*] speak, and are themselves part, of a legacy divided, as the dedications specify, between Warren's daughter Rosanna and son Gabriel."[5]

Freed from the conflict of his first marriage and presented with a fresh start and young children in his middle years, Warren doubtless felt a sense of renewal. The majority of the poems in *Promises* attest to his newfound ability to "look with joy upon the irremediable things," as he paraphrased Yeats in "A Conversation with Cleanth Brooks." That his children provided the most significant inspiration shows the extension of his vision toward the future. Although the developments in his personal life should not be discounted, his gradual movement toward the type of joy expressed in *Promises* demonstrates an important stylistic and aesthetic breakthrough. Warren's "whole new sense of poetry" brought together the two types of poetry he had been working on earlier in his career, the lyric modes as well as the ballad forms based on an element of narrative.[6] His intensive study

3. Warren, "Reminiscences," interview by Farrell, in *Talking with Robert Penn Warren*, ed. Watkins et al., 297.

4. See Blotner, *Robert Penn Warren*. Chapters 2–4 give the most detailed accounts of this twenty-year period in Warren's life.

5. Leonard Casper, *Robert Penn Warren: The Dark and Bloody Ground* (Seattle: University of Washington Press, 1960), 80.

6. Robert Penn Warren, "A Conversation with Cleanth Brooks," in *The Possibilities of Order: Cleanth Brooks and His Work*, ed. Lewis P. Simpson (Baton Rouge: Louisiana State University Press, 1976), 26; Warren, "Robert Penn Warren," interview by Walker, in *Talking with Robert Penn Warren*, ed. Watkins et al., 162.

of the English Romantics had clarified what his "yearning" temperament explored only hesitantly in his first collections of poetry and then peripherally in his criticism of the 1940s—the sense of hope and redemption and a heightened awareness of the interrelatedness of human experience. In *Promises*, Warren integrates the predominantly Romantic views he found so congenial to his temperament into his observations about his life and the natural world. The result is a powerful sequence of poems that, like Wordsworth's *Prelude*, moves beyond autobiography into a psychological penetration of the poetic imagination.

Unlike Eliot, who saw Romantic poetry as escapist, Warren understood that imaginative vision began first and foremost with the concrete. To render experience into abstract terms is, in many ways, a denial of the world itself, and Warren was, above all, a "creature of this world." As M. H. Abrams, Harold Bloom, C. M. Bowra, Jerome McGann, Geoffrey Hartman, and other Romantic scholars have illustrated, the Romantic theories of the imagination and epistemology focused on the external world. Poetry mediated the interaction between mind and object, passion and perception. In a similar fashion, Warren attributed his new outlook to his emphasis on the concrete. Prior to his poetic revival in the 1950s, he "had been into more abstract subjects," as he commented to interviewer Peter Stitt in 1977: " 'Billie Potts' was the last poem I wrote before the drought set in. It was a bridge piece, my jumping-off place when I started again, ten years later. Now my method is more mixed. Some poems start with a mood. The "mood" that Warren cites as the stimulus for his poems, particularly in *Promises*, strikingly resembles the governing Romantic metaphors of inspiration that he had explored and discussed in detail in his essay on *Rime of the Ancient Mariner*. In the same interview with Stitt, Warren applies these metaphors to describe his source of poetic inspiration: "Say there is a stream under your window, and you are aware of the sound all night as you sleep; or you notice the moonlight on the water, or hear an owl call. Things like this can start a mood that will carry over into the daylight. These objects may not appear in the poem, but the mood gets you going." The image of the stream as an emblem for the poetic imagination is one of the most

recurrent symbols in Romantic poetry. (Consider Wordsworth's reveries as he gazes upon the "sylvan Wye.")[7] In "A Poem of Pure Imagination," Warren discusses at length the importance of moonlight in
the Romantic aesthetic. He quotes Coleridge's remarks on how the
moonlight "changes the familiar world to make it poetry," thus
equating moonlight with "the modifying colours of the imagination"
(*SE*, 235). In his new approach to poetry, either consciously or uncon-
sciously, Warren invokes the Romantic conception of the symbolic
relevance of moonlight to define his newly awakened imaginative
powers.

Warren's "new outlook" in *Promises* forcefully affirms the rekin-
dling of the Romantic spark that his adherence to Eliot in his early
years, as well as his own depression, had suppressed. In many of the
poems, he juxtaposes his childhood memories with the present, linking the visions of childhood with the observations of the mature
mind. Throughout the series of poems, Warren struggles to reconcile
his personal vision, dimmed by time and experience, with the "visionary gleam" he remembers from his childhood and witnesses in the
lives of his children. Although the images of corruption and decay
that permeate his early poems still appear, an overall sense of hope
and joy emerges as a counterforce against the darker elements of
human experience.

The first poetic sequence in *Promises*, entitled "To a Little Girl,
One Year Old, in a Ruined Fortress," takes place in the Italian setting
that had special significance for Warren: "It was a very striking
place—there is a rocky peninsula with the sea on three sides, and a
sixteenth-century fortress on the top. . . . Seeing a little gold-headed
girl on that bloody spot of history is an *event*."[8] In "Sirocco," Warren
conveys this sense of the horrors of history balanced by his hope for

7. Bedient, *In the Heart's Last Kingdom*, 7; Warren, "An Interview with
Robert Penn Warren," by Stitt, in *Talking with Robert Penn Warren*, ed.
Watkins et al., 239; Wordsworth, "Lines Composed a Few Miles above Tin-
tern Abbey," in *Selected Poems and Prefaces*, ed. Stillinger, 109.

8. Warren, "An Interview with Robert Penn Warren, by Stitt, in *Talking
with Robert Penn Warren*, ed. Watkins et al., 239.

the future: "We have brought you where geometry of a military rigor survives its own ruined world, / And sun regilds your gilt hair, in the midst of your laughter" (*CP*, 103). The innocence of his young daughter counterbalances the poet's darkened vision of humanity and history. He has made his passage into the "ruined world" of time and experience and witnessed the frustrations of life, but his child has not.[9] Her laughter is like the sirocco, the wind of inspiration that intrudes into the poet's dispirited reflections on the futility of human effort. The poet looks upon the ruins of the ancient fortress and remembers Philip of Spain, a figure "For whom nothing prospered, though he loved God," but the child observes nothing but the beauty among the ruins—"Sun blaze and cloud tatter / . . . air like gold gauze whirled" (*CP*, 103).

In "Gull's Cry," the second poem of the Rosanna sequence, the child's laughter again delivers the poet from the temptations of naturalistic despair. The goat droppings, the defective child playing in the dirt, and the wife of the *gobbo* who "sits under vine leaves" all remind him of the anguish of the present (as opposed to the fruitlessness of the past he recalls in "Sirocco"), but at the sound of Rosanna's laughter, he is transported beyond the "molecular dance of the stone-dark": "And in that moment of possibility, let *gobbo*, *gobbo*'s wife, and us, and all, take hands and sing: redeem, redeem!" (*CP*, 103). In the blessing of his daughter's laughter, Warren reveals his discovery of the joy that may be found even in the most dismal surroundings.

It would be a mistake, however, to assume that the joyous conclusion of "Gull's Cry" suggests a complete negation of the "malfeasance of nature or the filth of fate" (*CP*, 104). The abrupt "blessing" at the end of "Gull's Cry" provides but a momentary stay against the ugliness of the world, making the concluding couplet indicative of a singular moment of redemptive vision, which must be re-earned each time the poet faces further evidence of suffering. Successively, in each of the five poems in the Rosanna sequence, the speaker confronts images that challenge the tentative affirmations reached in the preced-

9. Strandberg views the figure of Rosanna as "the vanished self returned from paradise, with Wordsworthian efficacy" (*Poetic Vision*, 64).

ing poems. Thus in poem III, "The Child Next Door," he appears to abandon the "glimmer of joy" to focus on the "defective" child next door, the "monstrous other" who stands in opposition to both the "golden-haired" Rosanna and the beautiful sister who watches the defective child. Rosanna is not mentioned directly in this poem, but she serves as an implied foil to the "monster" who has been taught "to make *ciao*, Italian-wise" (*CP*, 104).

Here, at the midpoint of the five-poem sequence, the poet must rely on his inward perception for a source of joy because there is no scenic beauty or child's laughter to dispel the squalidness that he observes. The capacity to love the world just as it is forms the crux of all of the poems in *Promises*. Therefore, the poet must, like the Ancient Mariner, move beyond the "hate" that initially seizes him toward an identification with what he feels compelled to despise. While the reverie of higher innocence that occupies the other poems of this sequence appears elusive, the speaker arrives at a hard-won acceptance of "heart-joy": "I think of your goldness, of joy, how empires grind, stars are hurled. / I smile stiff, saying *ciao*, saying *ciao*, and think: this is the world" (*CP*, 104). By responding to the child's gesture, Warren as poet acknowledges what Warren as critic earlier refers to in "A Poem of Pure Imagination" as the "sacramental vision" in which all living things participate (*SE*, 214). The gesture of *ciao* creates a connection between the child and the poet and enlarges his awareness that even in the inadequacy of language, the imperfectly communicated sign, the same joy and limitations bind them.

The next poem, "The Flower," offers a different perspective from that presented in the two preceding poems, "Gull's Cry" and "The Child Next Door." The latter poems thrust the reader into the "purlieu of dirt" that "is the world" (*CP*, 104), the ruined fortress and dirty village that represent failed human effort and ceaseless struggle. Redemption is available only through the sustained reconciliation of opposing forces. The squalor of the *gobbo*'s villa, the innocence of Rosanna's laughter, the defective child and its sister, and the poet himself are all a part of "the world," and the ritual of blessing manifests the poet's identification with the external world. "The Flower," much like "Sirocco," blends the poet's observations of nature with his consciousness of his daughter's more innocent perceptions. The main difference between "Sirocco," the first poem in the sequence, and "The Flower" is the vision the poet has gained in the poems that intervene between them.

The descriptions of nature in "The Flower" evoke a hymn-like quality of reverence:

> Bee-drowsy and blowsy with white bloom,
> Scarcely giving the passer-by room.
> We know that that blossomy mass
> Will brush our heads as we pass,
> And at knee there's gold gorse and blue clover,
> And at ankle, blue *malva* all over.

> (*CP*, 105)

The poet momentarily looks at nature as his child does, observing the lushness and the "scent and sun-honey of air" (*CP*, 105). Yet as Strandberg notes, "The basic flaw of this loveliest world is its transitoriness,"[10] and the poet, much like Wordsworth in his Intimations Ode and "Tintern Abbey," acknowledges the passage of time and its effects on man and his perception of nature. The child Rosanna, in her innocence, can "sing as though human need / Were not for perfection" (*CP*, 106), but the poet knows that although he can delight in his daughter's joy at even the most withered of blooms, he must ultimately serve as his daughter's guide to the world of time and experience.

John L. Stewart, Marshall Walker, and Leonard Casper have commented on the "technical deficiencies" of "The Flower." Walker has argued that this poem is the "least successful" in the Rosanna sequence because the short lines "are at odds with the poem's uneasy combination of narrative and meditation." However, I find that the short lines convey a sense of hesitancy wholly appropriate for the task the poet has before him:

10. Strandberg, *A Colder Fire*, 191

> I carry you up the hill.
> In my arms you are sweet and still.
> We approach your special place,
> And I am watching your face
> To see the sweet puzzlement grow,
> And then recognition glow.
> Recognition explodes in delight.
> You leap like spray, or like light.
>
> (*CP*, 105)

As parent and adult, the poet wants to prevent his daughter from experiencing the loss that accompanies maturity, yet "Despite [his] arm's tightness," the child "leap[s] in gold-glitter and brightness / . . . And reach[es] out" (*CP*, 105). Here Warren offers a perspective similar to Wordsworth's claim that "nothing can bring back the hour / Of splendour in the grass, of glory in the flower."[11] But Warren's viewpoint is directed toward his child and his awareness of the necessity of her initiation into time: "Yes, I'm well aware / That this is the spot, and hour, / For you to demand your flower" (*CP*, 105).

As he made clear in *Brother to Dragons*, Warren is not advocating a regression to childhood, but he does celebrate the child's freshness of perception as well as the adult's capacity to regain some of this visionary power through memory. In this way, he aligns himself with what M. H. Abrams calls the "major lyric innovation of the Romantic period . . . in which the poet confronts a particular scene at a significant stage of his life, in a colloquy that specifies the present, evokes the past, and anticipates the future." According to Hegel, "The harmoniousness of childhood is a gift from the hand of nature: the second harmony must spring from the labour and culture of the spirit."[12] By observing his daughter's delight in a flower, the poet can partly recover innocence. Thus, we have in Warren's poem "the glory

---

11. See Walker, *A Vision Earned*, 140; Wordsworth, "Ode: Intimations of Immortality from Recollections of Early Childhood," in *Selected Poems and Prefaces*, ed. Stillinger, 190.

12. Abrams, *Natural Supernaturalism*, 123; Hegel quoted *ibid.*, 380.

of the flower" as recollected by the adult, who through a child, can disimprison his lost sense of wonder.

Yet as an adult, despite his pleasure in watching his daughter, the poet remains aware of what Wordsworth calls "the still sad music of humanity":[13] "But the season has thinned out . . . The mountain prepares the night" (*CP*, 106). Time and experience have dimmed his eyes, yet the child's innocence compels him to "accept the incipient night" and offer an invocation of future hope:

> Let the future reassess
> All past joy, and past distress,
> Till we know Time's own deep intent,
> And the last integument
> Of the past shall be rent
> To show how all things bent
> Their energies to that hour
> When you first demanded your flower.
>
> (*CP*, 106)

Rosanna's "delight" evokes the poet's reveries as well as his consideration that she, too, will be subject to the diminution of vision he has suffered, but the mature narrator finds lessons applicable to his search for blessedness. Acceptance, not regression, provides the central focus of the poet's exploration, and in true Romantic fashion the poet consigns himself to the totality of life, time, and experience.

This renewed determination to find a way to live "despite all naturalistic considerations" inspires the "promise" in the fifth and last poem in the Rosanna sequence (*BD*, 21). In "Colder Fire," the development of perspective that occurs in each of the four earlier poems moves toward a final appraisal of the poet's search for "joy," even in the midst of the grim world he observes. This last poem in the sequence offers Warren's version of Wordsworth's "emotion recollected

13. Wordsworth, "Lines Composed a Few Miles above Tintern Abbey," in *Selected Poems and Prefaces*, ed. Stillinger, 110.

in tranquility," and its setting and method suggest the deliberate, meditative manner of the Romantic lyric. On a descriptive level, "Colder Fire" resembles Wordsworth's "Resolution and Independence." Wordsworth's poem begins, "There was a roaring in the wind all night; / The rain came heavily and fell in floods,"[14] whereas Warren's poem opens with "It rained toward day. The morning came sad and white / With silver of sea-sadness and defection of season" (*CP*, 107). In the manner of the Romantic *reverdie*, both poets welcome the passing of the storm and the emergence of the sun.[15] Wordsworth writes, "But now the sun is rising calm and bright; the birds are singing in the distant woods"; Warren describes the scene in a similar fashion: "Now sun, afternoon, and again summer-glitter on sea" (*CP*, 107). In both poems, all of nature participates in the same "heart's joy" that the speakers feel, allowing Wordsworth to observe with delight "The hare . . . running races in her mirth" and Warren to marvel at the "White butterflies over gold thistle [who] conduct their ritual carouse" (*CP*, 107).[16]

As much as the surface similarities between these two poems indicate Warren's evolution toward the Romantic concept of nature as a restorative agent, deeper and more compelling parallels arise through the poet's reflections. Wordsworth's speaker in "Resolution and Independence" cannot move blithely through the beauty of nature; he, like the speaker in "Tintern Abbey," is aware of the "still, sad music of humanity" and the precariousness of joy:

> As high as we have mounted in delight
> In our dejection do we sink as low;

14. Wordsworth, Preface to the Second Edition of *Lyrical Ballads*, *ibid.*, 460; "Resolution and Independence," *ibid.*, 165.

15. For both poets, however, the "storm" might also serve as a metaphor describing the power of imaginative passion, the "spontaneous overflow of emotion" that engenders poetry—turbulent and potentially destructive but integral to the creative act.

16. Wordsworth, "Resolution and Independence," in *Selected Poems and Prefaces*, ed. Stillinger, 165.

To me that morning did it happen so;
And fears and fancies thick upon me came;
Dim sadness—and blind thoughts, I knew not, nor could name.

The arbitrary and uncertain nature of joy also strikes Warren in "Colder Fire," for even though "The heart unlocks joy," he understands, "shamefaced, the heart's weather should not be / Merely a reflex to solstice, or sport of some aggrieved equinox" (*CP*, 107). This tentative joy must be earned through deep reflection and struggle. Warren, who found such happiness in his middle years, realized that this "aggrieved equinox" neither eradicated the past nor guaranteed an untarnished future. Rather, he draws on Wordsworth's idea of the "strength in what remains behind" (190), hoping to impart to his children both the delight and the peril in the search for meaning.[17]

In a mode similar to Yeats's "A Prayer for My Daughter," "Colder Fire" is Warren's poetic blessing for his daughter. Realizing that he cannot foresee or control his children's destinies, Warren extends his benediction, fraught with the burden of his experience. This ritual of blessing has antecedents in Wordsworth's "Tintern Abbey" and Coleridge's "Frost at Midnight." "Tintern Abbey" concludes with this blessing from the poet to his sister:

> . . . thy mind
> Shall be a mansion for all lovely forms,
> Thy memory be as a dwelling place
> For all sweet sounds and harmonies; oh! then,
> If solitude, or fear, or pain, or grief,
> Should be thy portion, with what healing thoughts
> Of tender joy whilt thou remember me,
> And these my exhortations![18]

Yeats continues this tradition in "A Prayer for My Daughter," lyrically evoking the innocence of childhood poised on the coming initi-

17. *Ibid.*, 166; Wordsworth, *Intimations Ode*, ibid., 190.
18. Wordsworth, "Lines Composed a Few Miles above Tintern Abbey," *ibid.*, 111.

ation into a world less than kind to those who, in Warren's words, "sing as though human need / Were not for perfection" (*CP*, 106). Warren progresses from the concrete beauty of nature to the abstract realm of memory, with his final vision culminating in a synthesis of his search for meaning and his hopes for the future. He also emphasizes the importance of memory, although he admits that he cannot "interpret" for his daughter "this collocation / Of memories" (*CP*, 108). Yet with his faith in the power of memory, the poet urges his daughter to follow "the language of [her] own heart," which "in the last analysis [will] be always of whatever truth" she would live (*CP*, 108).

The "colder fire" is the vision earned through a lifetime, dimmed by experience but maintained through memory. Wordsworth's heights of joy are not without their sloughs of despond, and Warren reaffirms this notion in his acknowledgment that "Height is not deprivation of valley, nor defect of desire," but in the end, the realized totality of vision "defines, for the fortunate, that joy in which all joys should rejoice" (*CP*, 108). To Warren, the "fortunate" are those who can, in Yeats's words, recover "radical innocence" ("radical" in the original sense of "rooted") despite the tragedies of life.[19] The five Rosanna poems in *Promises* emerge not only as the poet's "prayer" for his daughter but also as an affirmation of the joy he has struggled to discover.

In the second section of *Promises*, Warren extends the "collocation / Of memories" (*CP*, 108) to his son Gabriel. In this sequence, however, he focuses more on the landscape of his past than the Italian setting that inspires his Rosanna poems. The emphasis on memory that characterizes the Rosanna sequence also unifies the poems for Gabriel. Just as observi⸱ ⸱ "bloody spot of history" provokes Warren's contemplations of possibility despite the presence of human ruin, so does the birth of his son further enlarge his sense of the generational and historical links among past, present, and future. Warren offers a "collocation / Of memories" (*CP*, 108) in his poems to Gabriel, juxtaposing the remembered evanescence of boyhood with the harsh realities of nature and human weakness. Watching his children thrive during the time at Porto Ercole obviously spurred Warren's remembrances of his parents as well as his boyhood in Kentucky. As Justus observes, the power behind these poems lies in Warren's attempts "to comprehend the significance of remembered scenes, people, episodes."[20] Even as the poet perceives "our own time's sad declension" (*CP*, 120), he delves into the departed glory of history and the past to find significance, both for himself and for his children.

In the first poem of the Gabriel sequence, "What Was the Promise That Smiled from the Maples at Evening?", the speaker (whom we can assume is Warren) recalls watching older boys shoot bullbats. He is "Too little to shoot" the birds that "skimmer and skitter in gold light at great height," but he takes his first vicarious, initiative step toward knowledge as he picks up one of the dead birds: "Why, that's blood, it is wet. / Its eyes are still open, your heart in the throat swells like joy" (*CP*, 109). This moment of intense realization, reminiscent of the Romantic "spot of time," represents the boy's awareness not only of life and death but also of a more personal sense of mutability. Paradoxically, "joy" is coupled with a feeling of loss, and the boy flees the scene "on impulse," resisting his parents' calls as he hides "in darkness" (*CP*, 109). Warren had earlier written in "Revelation" that "In separateness only does love learn definition" (*CP*, 71), and the boy's reaction to the dead bird, so powerfully captured in the mature poet's memory, illuminates the convergence of love and knowledge, innocence and experience.

After this description of a revelatory moment from his boyhood, the mature poet considers "All the long years before" and how "after the dying was done / . . . Recollection of childhood was natural." Instead of initially realizing "intimations of immortality," he thinks of his parents' deaths as reminders of his own mortality, the "cold gust at the back." As the poet later stands "in a cold and coagulate evening" before the graves of his parents, he imagines the skeletal re-

20. Warren, "An Interview with Robert Penn Warren," in *Talking with Robert Penn Warren*, ed. Watkins et al., 239; Justus, *Achievement*, 72.

mains of Ruth and Robert Warren, "the fleshly habiliments rent— /
But agleam in a phosphorus of glory, bones bathed, there they lay, /
Side by side." Nature appears to offer no sustenance: ". . . the farms
and far woods fled away, / And a gray light prevailed and both landscape and heart were subdued" (*CP*, 109). Strandberg finds that such
a naturalistic rendering suggests the "essential isolation and inaccessi-
bility of the living from the dead." But characteristic of the "One
Life" theme that appears throughout *Promises*, Warren explores the
Romantic correlative between memory and nature to alleviate the
grief of loss. As is seen in *Rime*, natural and supernatural elements
combine to elicit human benediction; after the ghostly apparition of
his parents brings the poet into an awareness of continuity, he turns
his "gaze to that world which had once been the heart's familiar, /
Swell of woods and far field-sweep, in twilight by stream-gleam now
wefted / . . . far under the first star." Memory evokes meaning beyond
the finality of death. At the end of the poem, the poet hears his
mother's voice, "long forgotten, calm in silence," simply saying,
"Child"; his father's voice follows: "We died only that every promise
might be fulfilled" (*CP*, 104). Poised between memories of his life as
a child and his life as an adult and father, Warren stresses the importance of continuity against the temptations of deterministic resigna-
tion.

In "Fresh Air," a parody of "What Was the Promise That Smiled
from the Maples at Evening?," Kenneth Koch satirizes the poems in
Promises as self-indulgent nostalgia. Such a view, however, severely
underestimates how the poet has chosen to invoke the past. Even in
the most affirmative poems, which seem to offer the most explicit answers, the sincerity and humility of the poet's disclosures suggest that
the events described have meaning precisely because they resist ready
interpretation. The "promise" extended in "What Was That Promise
That Smiled from the Maples at Evening?" is one of the continuity
of love and discovery, yet its implications reveal further questions in
the poet's quest for meaning.[21]

21. Strandberg, *A Colder Fire*, 223; Kenneth Koch, "Fresh Air," in *Thank
You and Other Poems* (New York: Grove Press, 1962), 55.

From Warren's personal and historical perspective, the "calmness" of his parents' blessing is not to be undervalued, especially given the turbulence of past and present history. Despite the transitory "heart-joy" (*CP*, 104) he ascertains and wishes to impart to his son, the world Warren presents is fraught with violence and danger that threaten to annihilate any vestiges of innocence. In "Court-martial" (poem II), one of Warren's remembrances of his grandfather Gabriel Penn, the grandson listens to his grandfather's accounts of hanging "bush-whackers" during the Civil War. The boy seeks, "somehow, to untie / The knot of History" (*CP*, 111), and he has difficulty reconciling the old man who sits before him "now shrunken, gray" with the "Captain, cavalry, C. S. A." who took part in violent and bloody war. When the boy apparently looks questioningly at his grandfather, the old man cries, "By God, they deserved it / . . . Don't look at me that way" (*CP*, 112). The boy, however, can only relate to the immediate world he knows; he "snatche[s]" his gaze away and returns to the world of nature, "the blazing day" and the "far woods" (*CP*, 112). But the voice of the poet, grown wiser in his later years, revisits this memory and is able to understand more clearly how dignity—a way to live—can be constructed even in the face of

> mortgage and lien and debt,
> Cutworm and hail and drouth,
> Bang's disease, hoof-and-mouth,
> Barn sagging and broken house.
>
> (*CP*, 110)

The lesson he learns transcends the inexplicable necessity of brutality, yet Warren does not avert his eyes from the human potential for violence and depravity. Rather, he focuses on how the "*done* and the *to-be-done* / In that timelessness were one" (*CP*, 111) and discovers that "The world is real. It is there" (*CP*, 113).

Warren's chief discovery in the Gabriel poems, as in the Rosanna sequence, is an affirmative vision of the world, even when the speakers are confronted with seemingly mindless slaughter and destruction. Walker maintains that Warren's assessment of such a world is "at once both grim and tender," revealing an awareness of human complicity coupled with the capacity for sympathy. This capacity for sympathy, as Warren writes in his study of Coleridge is a celebration of "the chain of love which binds human society together, and the universe" (*SE*, 255), an affirmation of the "One Life" that links all of nature and humankind. Achieving such sympathy, however, is never easy, especially in the horrific world of "School Lesson Based on Word of Tragic Death of Entire Gillum Family," in which a father slaughters his family with an icepick. The students at the schoolhouse who hear of the mass murder of the Gillum children learn a "lesson" far more immediate and concrete than the "intellectual dream" of their studies:

> Though we studied and studied, as hard as we could, to know,
> Studying the arithmetic of losses,
>> To be prepared when the next one,
> By fire, flood, foe, cancer, thrombosis,
>> Or Time's slow malediction, came to be undone.
>
> (CP, 118–19)

Just as the speaker in Wordsworth's poem "The Thorn" cannot interpret the meaning behind a young woman's murder of her infant ("I cannot tell how this may be"), Warren's speaker does not try to explain away the inexplicable.[22] Initiated into a world in which parents kill their children, the young speaker must contend with the specter of irrationality and even evil as a necessary part of the human condition.

"School Lesson Based on Word of Tragic Death of Entire Gillum Family" addresses the problem of evil in its darkest and most sinister manifestations. The Romantic precepts so prevalent in many of the other poems in *Promises* appear remote in this poem. There are none of Wordsworth's reveries or Blake's apocalyptic visions, none of Shel-

---

22. Walker, *A Vision Earned*, 145; Wordsworth, "The Thorn," in *Selected Poems and Prefaces*, ed. Stillinger, 76.

ley's glimpses into the supernal or Keats's revelations of Truth and
Beauty. Yet the Romantics did address the problem of evil, and
M. H. Abrams defends the Romantics' central and pervasive concern
with human evil and suffering: "Finding no longer tenable the justification of earthly suffering as a divine plan for sorting out those beings who will be translated to a better world, they undertook to justify
the experience of suffering within the limits of experience itself."
Similarly, Warren's Romantic affirmations throughout *Promises* do
not ignore the agony and strife of human hearts. Like the Romantics,
Warren seeks to evoke what Abrams defines as "the tragic paradox
. . . that the values of life are valuable precisely because they are limited and defined by death."[23] By "Studying the arithmetic of losses"
(*CP*, 119), the schoolchildren in Warren's poem realize how death,
even taken out of the natural context, plays a role in their development as fully conscious and mature human beings. Yet the lesson of
the Gillums' tragic deaths is just the beginning of many lessons: "*We
studied all afternoon, till getting on to sun. / There was another lesson,
but we were too young to take up that one* [original emphasis]" (*CP*,
119). Time and experience will provide further episodes to challenge
and destroy the innocence of the children, but as Warren illustrates
earlier, in *Brother to Dragons*, a "new definition" of innocence leads
to a "sacramental vision of the universe" (*SE*, 249): "The recognition
of complicity is the beginning of innocence" (*BD* [1953], 214).

While "School Lesson Based on Word of Tragic Death of Entire
Gillum Family" is presumably based on an event from Warren's personal past, "Founding Fathers, Nineteenth-Century Style, Southeast
U.S.A." extends the scope to the poet's larger historical past. The
speaker reflects on not only famous historical figures (Jefferson,
Houston, Bowie, and Clay) who "stare from daguerreotype with se-
vere reprehension . . . / Or from genuine oil" with "merciless eyes
that now remark our own time's sad declension" but also "the name-
less, of whom no portraits remain" (*CP*, 120–21). The speaker in this
poem, much like R.P.W. in *Brother to Dragons* and the speaker in

23. Abrams, *Natural Supernaturalism*, 444.

"Court-martial," acknowledges the imperfections of the country's "Founding Fathers," but these shortcomings are not the focus of the poem. Warren's primary assertion that these "founders" "were human, they suffered" (*CP*, 120) connects this poem thematically with such other poems as "What Was the Promise That Smiled from the Maples at Evening?" and "School Lesson Based on Word of Tragic Death of Entire Gillum Family," in which Warren's Romantic conception of Coleridge's "One Life within us and Abroad" presents an image of humanity bound in the communion of both joy and suffering. Coleridge wrote in *The Friend* that "Man sallies forth into nature," only to learn "at last that what he seeks he has left behind." Warren, as with his Romantic predecessors, insists on the total process of history and experience. Just as Wordsworth's *Prelude* takes its power from the continuous dialectic between history and personal growth—what Karl Kroeber designates as the "objective drama" of history and the "subjective drama" of psychological exploration[24]— Warren's poem offers an entreaty for reconciliation: "So let us bend ear to them in this hour of lateness, / And what they are trying to say, try to understand" (*CP*, 121). Warren stresses that all of humanity is bound by the same "defects" and "greatness" that characterized the makers of history, "For we are their children in the light of humanness, and under the shadow of / God's closing hand" (*CP*, 121).

Warren's imaginative excursions into the past, both personal and historical, contain some of the more gruesome scenes that appear in his poetry, but set against these images of violence and futility are the lyrical evocations of childhood innocence in "Gold Glade." Again he returns to the "Tintern Abbey" of his youth, "the woods of boyhood, / Where cedar, black, thick, rode the ridge, / Heart aimless as rifle, boy-blankness of mood" (*CP*, 113). In a moment reminiscent of Wordsworth's "spots of time" in *The Prelude*, the boy in the poem enters a gorge and becomes transfixed by a glade, "geometric, circular, gold" (*CP*, 113). In this moment the boy senses the sublime infinitude of nature "Beyond any heart-hurt, or eye's grief-fall." Time is

24. Samuel Taylor Coleridge, *The Friend*, in *Samuel Taylor Coleridge*, ed. Jackson, 631; Kroeber, *Romantic Narrative Art*, 88–89.

suspended, and amid the "gold light" of the glade, "There could be
no dark" (*CP*, 113). Of course, as in the Romantic experience, the dark
does come. The speaker ages, loses his "visionary gleam," and even
has difficulty remembering the exact location of his childhood reverie: ". . . I can't recall / What county it was, for the life of me / . . .
Was it even Kentucky or Tennessee? / Perhaps just an image that
keeps haunting me" (*CP*, 113). Yet the Wordsworthian consolation,
the "abundant recompense" of a partial recovery of vision, sustains
the speaker even after his loss of innocence. Although imagination
and memory ultimately help the speaker retain his moment of vision,
the image is rooted in the concreteness of nature:

> . . . in no mansion under earth,
> Nor imagination's domain of bright air,
> But solid in soil that gave its birth,
> It stands, wherever it is, but somewhere.
> I shall set my foot, and go there.
>
> (*CP*, 113)

Like the Romantics, Warren insists that the mysticism of the "time-
less moment" is grounded in reality. This poem furnishes what
Strandberg calls a "private sanctuary of the soul," but it is ultimately
the "solid . . . soil" that elicits the speaker's sudden illumination.[25]
    The lyrical presentation of threshing time in the Kentucky of
Warren's youth supplies the setting for a thematically similar group-
ing of poems, "Boy's Will, Joyful Labor without Pay, and Harvest
Home" (1918), in which the poet again reflects on childhood events.
Secure in his Wordsworthian "glad animal movements" and his igno-
rance of time's "infinite constriction," the boy hurries to greet the
day:

> You bolt your oatmeal, up and go.
> The world is panting, the world won't wait.

25. See Strandberg, *A Colder Fire*, 224.

All energy's unregenerate.
Blood can't abide the status quo.

(*CP*, 139)

As the boy works alongside the men in the field, he upturns a snake's hiding place, and the "Men shout, ring around. He can't get away" (*CP*, 139). Like "fat old" *obsoleta* in *Brother to Dragons*, the black snake in this poem serves much the same symbolic function as the Mariner's sea snakes. It is recognizably a symbol of evil, representative of the primary agent of Original Sin and mankind's expulsion from paradise. Yet it is also a part of the "One Life"—the unitary nature of nature, with good and evil inextricably linked—that Warren emphasizes throughout *Promises*. The "detached" old man kills the snake, "Spits once," and says, "Hell, just another snake" (*CP*, 140), violating what Warren refers to earlier in "A Poem of Pure Imagination" as the "sacramental conception of the universe, by making man's convenience the measure of an act," thus isolating him from "Nature and the 'One Life'" (*SE*, 232).

The significance of this act does not immediately strike the boy, but unlike the old man, he is not "detached." He stores the event in his memory, and the poet's contemplation on this incident extends into the last poem of the sequence, "Hands Are Paid" (*CP*, 140). All that remains of the snake is a "little blood that smeared the stone," but the power of the image evokes the poet's reconsideration of the scene in his memory. The same "white star" that shone over him as a boy still beckons him as an adult, as he thinks how "the years go by like a breath, or eye-blink, / And all history lives in the head again." In his imagination, he can "see that scene, / And name each item, but cannot think / What, in their urgency, they must mean" (*CP*, 140), but it is not so much the "meaning" of the memories that become important as the effect that they have upon him. We are reminded of the actual Italian frame-setting of the poems in *Promises*, as the poet remarks that he "know[s], even now, on this foreign shore, / In blaze of sun and sea's stare, / A heart-stab blessed past joy or despair," and he sees, in his imagination, "in the mind's dark, once more, / That field, pale, under starlit air" (*CP*, 141). In this emphasis on the reconciling capacity of the imagination, Warren shares with the Romantics the belief that the landscape of memory can offer "Abundant recompense," if only a brief and fleeting insight into the worlds wrought by imagination and experience.[26]

Not all of the poems in *Promises* depict a world so firmly rooted in reality. Amid the scenes of memory, history, and the present exists "Dragon Country," where a mythical creature terrorizes the inhabitants of rural Kentucky. The people of "Dragon Country" at first attempt to explain away the "depredation[s]" of the dragon, preferring to blame the acts of destruction on rational and natural agencies. "It must be a bear," they say, but knowing that "no bear had been seen in the county in fifty years," the speaker realizes "It was something to say, merely that, for people compelled to explain / What, standing in natural daylight, they agreed couldn't be true" (*CP*, 133). Common sense, logic, and even science fail to explain the phenomenon. In this poem the literal is of almost no consequence, and the symbolic seizes precedence. Warren's employment of the symbolic through supernatural elements, much like Coleridge's explanation of his use of the supernatural in *Lyrical Ballads*, requires the same "willing suspension of disbelief." Whereas Wordsworth and Coleridge separated their poetic tasks in *Lyrical Ballads* into two "classes," the supernatural and "subjects . . . chosen from ordinary life,"[27] Warren incorporates both elements into his poem. He creates a rural environment that is suddenly plunged into violence and terror, not at the hands of a human being, as in "School Lesson Based on Word of Tragic Death of Entire Gillum Family," but from a beast whose existence defies every notion of order and belief.

Challenging the modern assumption that all events in nature are explainable through intellectual and scientific knowledge, Warren seeks in this poem to restore a sense of mystery to human life. The entirety of the title, "Dragon Country: To Jacob Boehme," alludes to

26. Wordsworth, "Lines Composed a Few Miles above Tintern Abbey," in *Selected Poems and Prefaces*, ed. Stillinger, 110.

27. Coleridge, *Biographia Literaria*, in *Samuel Taylor Coleridge*, ed. Jackson, 314.

the seventeenth-century German mystic and theologian whose ideas were integral to the development of the Romantic theory of "united and divided man" and who maintained that without contraries, there is no progression: "The reader should know that all things consist in Yes or No, whether these things are divine, devilish, earthly, or whatever else might be mentioned. . . . The No is the opponent of the Yes, or of truth, in order that the truth may become apparent. . . . Except for these two things, which nonetheless remain in constant conflict, all things would be a nothing, and would stand still and motionless." According to Strandberg, "The allusion to Jacob Boehme indicates the narrator's intention to impose upon a modern setting the medieval-Renaissance world-view, whereby happenings in this world are regarded as having other-worldly significance."[28] Instead of declaring the forces of good and evil mutually exclusive, Boehme stressed the necessity of tension between them. Warren's allegory points toward the same idea postulated by Boehme and much later by Blake and Coleridge: without mystery, without "Otherness," however terrifying, "all things would be a nothing, and would stand still and motionless." Like the Romantics, Warren emphasizes the need for the inexplicable. Science, modern man's greatest tool of rationalization, cannot solve the problem of evil by reducing it to mere deviation in the overall formula of the known universe.

Ridiculed by the outside world and unable to explain the dragon's presence, the townspeople in "Dragon Country" turn to religion in hopes of vanquishing the evil, but as the speaker says, "That's not the point": "We are human, and the human heart / Demands language for reality that has no slightest dependence / On desire, or need" (*CP*, 134). Even though "in church fools pray only that the Beast depart," the speaker stresses the "necessity of truth":

But if the Beast were withdrawn now, life might dwindle again
To the ennui, the pleasure, and the night sweat, known in the time before

28. Jacob Boehme quoted in Abrams, *Natural Supernaturalism*, 502, n. 36. See also Strandberg, *A Colder Fire*, 231.

Necessity of truth had trodden the land, and our hearts, to pain,
And left, in darkness, the fearful glimmer of joy, like a spoor.

(*CP,* 134)

Working in dialectical fusion, fear and joy become inextricable. As
Cleanth Brooks points out, "Admitting the element of horror in life,
conceding the element of mystery, facing the terrifying truth—these
are the only actions that can promise the glimmer of ultimate joy."[29]
Rationalization through science, denial, and religion may be the only
tools available in the face of the unknown, yet as "Dragon Country:
To Jacob Boehme" reveals, the polarities of good and evil are essential
to the awareness of joy.

Interspersed among images of his own childhood idylls and the
wanton destruction created by natural or supernatural forces are the
lyrics in which the poet specifically addresses his son. Gabriel was
only an infant when the poems in *Promises* were written, and the
times that he is mentioned in the poems, he is sleeping in his crib
with his father watching over him, much in the fashion of Coleridge's
"Frost at Midnight" and Yeats's "A Prayer for My Daughter." In
"When the Century Dragged," the first section of "Infant Boy at
Midcentury," the poet hopes that his son will eventually

> . . . pause, in high pride of undisillusioned manhood,
> At the gap that gives on the new century, and land,
> And with calm heart and level eye command
> That dawning perspective and possibility of human good.
>
> (*CP,* 126)

This benediction is not without its warnings, however, for the poet
tells his son that he "enters an age when the neurotic clock-tick / Of
midnight competes with the heart's pulsed assurance of power" (*CP,*
125). Yeats expresses similar fears in his poem to his daughter, a "great
gloom" caused by imagining "That the future years had come, / Dan-
cing to a frenzied drum, / Out of the murderous innocence of the

29. Brooks, "Afterword," 106–12.

sea." Significantly, in his poetic collection *Michael Robartes and the Dancer*, Yeats placed "A Prayer for My Daughter" immediately after "The Second Coming," which presents a nightmarish world where "the worst," full of "passionate intensity," seems ready to rule the earth while good men, grown skeptical, "lack all conviction."[30] Warren's own unheroic "age," an especially unstable one considering the sustained threat of nuclear annihilation, is "scarcely" the world's "finest hour," and "Good and Evil" pose for pictures and stage summits "to iron out all differences" (*CP*, 125). In the second poem, "Modification of Landscape," the speaker expresses the prospect of the next generation's "human heart-hope, and hand-scope" (*CP*, 126), but these descendants, too, must endure the same vicissitudes of their ancestors, "for flesh will yet grieve on the bone": "Yes, the new age will need the old lies, as our own once did." In "Brightness of Distance," the speaker asks for the same forgiveness for past errors sought in "Founding Fathers," urging his son to "Remember our defects, we give them to you gratis" (*CP*, 127).

Despite his misgivings about the future, the poet offers his son what blessing he can summon in the form of various "lullaby" poems. Central to these poems as well as Coleridge's "Frost at Midnight" is the major Romantic conception of memory as salvation, the theme that unifies all of the poems in *Promises*. Coleridge's "Abstruser musings" over his sleeping son invoke images from his past, and through memory he travels back to his childhood. In his discussion of "Frost at Midnight" in *The Visionary Company: A Reading of English Romantic Poetry*, Harold Bloom asserts that after these moments of imaginative recall, "the poet by associative progression is prepared to brood on the future of his slumbering infant."[31] Warren's "abstruser musings" are recorded in the poems that surround the "lullaby" poems, and although the threat of violence and decay is not absent ("You will, of course, see all / The world's brute ox-heel wrong, and

30. William Butler Yeats, *Selected Poems and Three Plays*, ed. M. L. Rosenthal (New York: Collier Books, 1986), 89.

31. Coleridge, "Frost at Midnight," in *Samuel Taylor Coleridge*, ed. Jackson, 87; Bloom, *Visionary Company*, 233.

shrewd hand-harm. / Throats are soft to invite the blade"), the over-all tone is one of gentleness and hope (*CP,* 128).

In "Frost at Midnight," Coleridge's blessing to his son signifies the restorative power of nature and the imagination: "Therefore all seasons shall be sweet to thee, / Whether the summer clothe the general earth / With greenness, or the redbreast sit and sit / Betwixt the tufts of snow on the bare branch / Of mossy apple-tree. . . ." Yeats evokes a similar image in "A Prayer for My Daughter," hoping that his child may "become a flourishing hidden tree . . . Rooted in one dear perpetual place."[32] Likewise, Warren invites his son to "Dream perfection" in "Lullaby: Smile in Sleep." That "perfection" is ultimately apotheosized in the world of nature:

> Dream that sleep is a sunlit meadow
> Drowsy with a dream of bees
> Threading sun, and the shadow
> Where you lie lulled by their sunlit industries.
>
> . . .
>
> Heart-deep now, your dreams will keep
> Sweet in that deep comb for time to come.
> Dream the sweetness coming on.
>
> (*CP,* 128)

Warren's blessing calls forth the same idyllic natural scenes detailed in "The Flower" ("Bee drowsy and blowsy with white bloom") (*CP,* 105), connecting the poems dedicated to both children with a mutual benediction.

In this poem and in "Lullaby: Moonlight Lingers," the moon appears as a symbol of memory and the imagination, which reflects Warren's statements concerning *Promises* and his rejuvenated poetic powers. The Rosanna poems are drenched in sunlight, while the poems tendered directly to Gabriel take place under the "cold moon

32. Coleridge, "Frost at Midnight," in *Samuel Taylor Coleridge,* ed. Jackson, 89; Yeats, "A Prayer for My Daughter," in *Selected Poetry,* ed. Webb, 126.

that is your dream's command" (*CP,* 128). In evaluating the importance of moonlight in Coleridge's *Rime,* Warren notes the specifically symbolic content of the "transfiguring light" of the moon. He cites I. A. Richards's definition of the function of moonlight throughout Coleridge's poetry: "When a writer has found a theme or image which fixes a point of relative stability in the drift of experience, it is not to be expected that he will avoid it. Such themes are a means of orientation" (*SE,* 234). According to Warren, the moon functions in connection with the theme of the imagination, meaning the imagination in "its value-creating capacity, what Coleridge was later to call the secondary imagination" (*SE,* 236).

Another passage from Coleridge becomes particularly significant in regard to Warren's similar use of moonlight in "Lullaby." Coleridge and Wordsworth, discussing their projected *Lyrical Ballads,* agreed "on the two cardinal points of poetry, the power of exciting the sympathy of the reader by a faithful adherence to the truth of nature, and the power of giving the interest of novelty by the modifying colours of the imagination." The "sudden charm" of moonlight, "diffused over a known and familiar landscape, appeared to represent the practicability of combining both."[33] To compound further Coleridge's use of moon symbolism, Warren cites a passage from Coleridge's *Anima Poetiae*: "In looking at objects of nature while I am thinking, as at yonder moon dim-glimmering through the dewy window-pane, I seem rather to be seeking, as it were asking for, a symbolic language for something within that always and forever exists, than observing anything new" (*SE,* 236). Warren's "symbolic language" of moonlight in "Lullaby" links past and present, conveying to the poet's mind "that landscape lost in the heart's homely deep" (*CP,* 131). The moonlight also gives "Dark secondary definition to the olive leaf," another allusion to Coleridge's theory of the secondary imagination that, as "an echo of the infinite I AM," recreates and unifies all objects in nature.

As the moonlight shines on his sleeping son, the poet thinks how

33. Coleridge, *Biographia Literaria,* in *Samuel Taylor Coleridge,* ed. Jackson, 314.

this same moonlight "fell in far times and other places," and "now in memory's stasis / I see moonlight mend an old man's Time-crossed brow" (*CP*, 132). Here moonlight is, quite literally, moonlight, but it also serves as the symbol of imagination and memory, reconciling the past with the present as well as the future embodied in Warren's sleeping son. Moonlight also provides what Bloom designates as "the imaginative unity" at the close of Coleridge's "Frost at Midnight" and is "emblematic both of creative joy and of the One Life of the phenomenal universe."[34] The movement from the speaker's meditation on his life to the blessing he extends to his son in Warren's "lullaby" poems has antecedents not only in Coleridge's "Frost at Midnight" but also, as mentioned before, in Wordsworth's "Tintern Abbey," especially in the lines, "Therefore let the moon / Shine on thee in thy solitary walk."[35] Warren's use of moonlight, however, does not suggest merely an appropriation of a prevalent Romantic symbol. Rather, moonlight becomes an expression of a style and attitude that Warren shared with the Romantics. Warren's lexicon of "symbolic language," increasingly influenced by the Romantics as his career progressed, links his inward apprehensions with the outward world he describes. Like Coleridge, Warren sought a "symbolic language for something within that always and forever exists." In *Promises*, that "something" is ultimately the joy that can be extracted from life.

The "lullaby" poems end with "Lullaby: A Motion Like Sleep," which offers the poet's final benediction to his son, the hope that he will grow and realize "How . . . deep, / Is Time's irremediable joy" (*CP*, 141). Yet this joy is also "like a wound," revealing the poet's

34. Bloom, *Visionary Company*, 205.

35. Wordsworth, "Lines Composed a Few Miles above Tintern Abbey," in *Selected Poems and Prefaces*, ed. Stillinger, 111. Bloom notes that "the closing paragraph of Coleridge's poem, directed to his infant son, beginning 'Therefore all seasons shall be sweet to thee,' is a prelude to the closing lines of 'Tintern Abbey,' where the poet asks nature's blessing on his sister." "Frost at Midnight" is dated February 1798; "Tintern Abbey" was composed on July 13, 1798.

awareness that the vision of joy, like anything else worthwhile in life, must be sought after despite the loss inherent in experience. Stewart contends in his discussion of *Promises* that Warren "was somewhat unskilled in the poetry of happiness" and found it "most difficult to write," yet the "lullaby" poems in particular show Warren's growing hopefulness despite his skepticism. The sun and moon, so often indicative in Warren's earlier poetry of naturalistic indifference (what Stewart labels "the grinding, bloody agony of the spheres" and "the ineffable sadness of the deprived heart"), become counterparts rather than counterforces in the dialectic upheaval.[36] As Casper observes, "The day of creation is shared by, rather than divided between, the newest generation, girl:sun and boy:moon whose prophetic radiance replaces those torrents of blinding guilt that drench the conscience in *Eleven Poems on the Same Theme*."[37] The last poem in *Promises*, "The Necessity for Belief," summarizes Warren's basic premise throughout the volume, the turning toward nature to discover examples of quiet acceptance:

> The sun is red, and the sky does not scream.
>
> . . .
>
> There is much that is scarcely to be believed.
>
> . . .
>
> The moon is in the sky, and there is no weeping.
> Much is told that is scarcely to be believed.
>
> (*CP*, 142)

The calmness that Warren emphasizes in "What Was the Promise That Smiled from the Maples at Evening?" comes full circle in "The Necessity for Belief." Memory, imagination, and a sense of continuity lead to the speaker's declaration in "Ballad of a Sweet Dream of Peace": "You fool, poor fool, all Time's a dream, and we're all one Flesh, at last" (*CP*, 136). In "The Return: An Elegy," one of Warren's

36. See Stewart, *Burden of Time*, 523, 519.
37. Casper, *Robert Penn Warren*, 81.

early poems, the speaker despairs over the "dry essential of tomorrow" (*CP*, 35). In *Promises*, the vision of the future is much more hopeful. One by one, these poems document Warren's search for the "joy in which all joys should rejoice" (*CP*, 108).

In the years immediately following the publication of *Promises*, Warren devoted his energies to poetry as well as to other genres, producing a collection of essays, three novels (*The Cave, Wilderness*, and *Flood*), a play version of *All the King's Men*, and two nonfiction works, *The Legacy of the Civil War* and *Who Speaks for the Negro?*. His new poetic volumes included *You, Emperors, and Others: Poems, 1957–1960, Tale of Time: New Poems, 1960–1966* (first published in *Selected Poems: New and Old, 1923–1966*), and *Incarnations: Poems, 1966–1968.* Such prolific output in nearly every genre testifies to Warren's renewed creative powers, and either directly or indirectly, each work after 1957 reveals the evolution of his Romantic vision. The poems in *Promises* projected the direction that Warren's poetry as well as his fiction would take, and his novels of this period recapitulate the most prominent themes that emerge in his post-drought poetry. Of particular importance is the anguished struggle toward an "osmosis of being" ("Knowledge," 185), a reconciliation of past ideals with a new vision of selfhood. Jack Harrick of *The Cave*, Adam Rosensweig of *Wilderness*, and Brad Tolliver of *Flood* are among the fortunate few in Warren's fiction who achieve the self-transcending vision necessary for their private salvation. Yet, like the writer himself, they find that any blessedness the world might have to offer must be earned only through the most painful and costly excursions into the past, the self that was, and the self that is to be.

Warren's fiction explores the issues of self-knowledge that exist at the heart of all of his work, but he speaks most revealingly and personally in his poems. In *You, Emperors, and Others* and *Tale of Time*, Warren returns to the "landscape lost in the heart's homely deep," each volume offering an evaluation of the emotions occasioned by his parents' deaths. Despite the intensely private nature of these poems, Warren emphasizes the universal need for understanding and the joy that exists "In the heart's last kingdom" (*CP*, 158). Even amid the nightmarish sections of *Incarnations,* which unflinchingly depict a death-row inmate's final battle with cancer and an elderly black woman's death in a hit-and-run accident, Warren juxtaposes the grimness of life with the tentatively affirmative notion that "We must try / To love so well the world that we may believe, in the end, in God" (*CP*, 233). This yearning for a way to live "Amid History's vice and velleity" (*CP*, 158), as Warren writes in "Fox-Fire: 1956," provides the impulse for his later poetry, especially for what many consider his finest work, *Audubon: A Vision*. In the next chapter I discuss how Warren's idea for "a long poem on Audubon," a project that began in the 1940s, evolved into his most fully realized Romantic vision.[38]

38. Clark and Warren, "Interview with Eleanor Clark and Robert Penn Warren," interview by Newquist, in *Talking with Robert Penn Warren*, ed. Watkins et al., 333.

IV

Coleridge Revisited

Robert Penn Warren's *Audubon: A Vision*, published in 1969, captured the attention of the literary world and reaffirmed Harold Bloom's assessment of Warren as a poet "who has taken on his full power over language and the world of the senses." Instead of experiencing a decline in poetic powers during his later years, Warren seemed to reach the height of his mastery. T. R. Hummer, emphasizing the continuity of Warren's poetic development, argues that the book is a "summation of everything Warren had been struggling with through the course of his career." Calvin Bedient even suggests that Warren's "greatness as a writer . . . began with *Audubon: A Vision*." Several early reviews of the poem praised Warren's masterful adaptation of John James Audubon's journals and writings, and critics such as Louis Martz and Allen Shepherd examined his transformation of Audubon's prose into a psychological exploration of the ornithologist's life and writings.[1] The full import of Warren's title, however, suggests

1. In his introduction to *Modern Critical Views: Robert Penn Warren*, Harold Bloom admits that "other critics of Warren's poetry see more continuity in development than I do. But in 1968 I was a belated convert, transported against my will by reading *Incarnations*" (5). See also T. R. Hummer, "Robert Penn Warren: Audubon and the Moral Center," *Southern Review* 16 (autumn

the suspension of strictly historical considerations in favor of the poet's imaginative rendering—his "vision." This vision of the solitary artist who seeks to confirm both his identity and his ideals through art and nature has its roots in Warren's developing Romanticism. Since Warren's study of the English Romantic poets in the 1940s figures so centrally in the development of his criticism as well as in his evolving ideas about his craft, *Audubon* can be seen as both an outgrowth and an indicator of Warren's Romantic vision. In this work a decidedly Romantic mythos emerges, one that is adapted to the American terrain both literally and figuratively.

When Peter Stitt asked Warren in 1977 how he came to write his "beautiful poem," Warren replied that his interest in the historical Audubon stemmed from his research for the novel *World Enough and Time* and his exploration of "Americana of the early nineteenth century [and] histories of Kentucky and Tennessee." Intrigued by Audubon's role in these histories, Warren "got interested in the man and his life, and began, way back in the forties, to write a poem about [him]." Drawing from the five-volume *Ornithological Biography*, Warren chose portions of its sixty "Episodes" as the historical foundation of the poem. His interest in Audubon as a significant figure in American history, particularly Audubon's role in what Justus calls "America's mythologizing impulse," provided him with the necessary subject matter. However, as Ruppersburg points out in *Robert Penn Warren and the American Imagination*, the central figure in Warren's poem is "a construct of the poet's imagination, a fusion of historical fact and imaginative vision where vision seizes precedence."[2] Like Yeats, Warren seeks to create a myth for his age, and this myth takes its form and substance from the Romantic tradition. *Audubon* com-

1980): 803–10; Bedient, *In the Heart's Last Kingdom*, 3; Louis L. Martz, "Recent Poetry: Established Idiom," *Yale Review* 59 (1970): 566; Allen Shepherd, "Warren's *Audubon*: 'Issue in Purer Form' and 'The Ground Rules of Fact,' " *Mississippi Quarterly* 24 (winter 1970): 47–56.

2. Warren, "An Interview with Robert Penn Warren," interview by Stitt, in *Talking with Robert Penn Warren*, ed. Watkins et al., 243–44. See also Justus, *Achievement*, 89, and Ruppersburg, *American Imagination*, 79.

bines Warren's concern with autobiographical self-recognition and the dynamics of memory with a heroic figure whose fidelity to his artistic ideals asserts the power of imaginative activity over the tyranny of material illusion.

Warren's "vision" of Audubon takes certain liberties with the historical sources. In the foreword to the 1953 version of *Brother to Dragons*, a poem similar to *Audubon* in its attention to historical personages, Warren explains his modifications: "I am trying to write a poem and not a history, and therefore have no compunction about tampering with facts. But poetry is more than fantasy and is committed to the obligation of trying to say something about the human condition. Therefore a poem dealing with history is no more at liberty to violate what the writer takes to be the spirit of his history than it is at liberty to violate what the writer takes to be the nature of the human heart" (*BD* [1953], xii). Warren goes on to say, "Historical sense and poetic sense should not, in the end, be contradictory, for if poetry is the little myth we make, history is the big myth we live, and in our living, constantly remake" (*BD* [1953], xii). In his personal life, *Brother to Dragons* marked the end of his poetic "dry spell," as he later called it, and signaled his forceful return to the poetic arena. During his poetic drought of the 1940s, Warren had conceived the idea for "a long poem on Audubon," but as he told Stitt in 1977, "it wouldn't come together, so I set it aside and forgot about it." In another interview of the 1970s, Warren cited *Audubon* as one of his "easy" poems, an assessment that may appear surprising considering its twenty-five-year evolution. By the time Warren finished the poem in 1969, he had published four volumes of poetry, five novels, and a collection of essays. While the poetry and fiction written during the 1950s and 1960s address many of the dominant issues and themes that later emerge in *Audubon*, the critical essays of the 1940s reveal a great deal about the sources that influenced the creation of the poem. Strandberg asserts that the most powerful of Warren's essays from the 1940s—"Pure and Impure Poetry" (1942), "Love and Separateness in Eudora Welty" (1944), "Melville the Poet" (1945), and "A Poem of Pure Imagination" (1945–46)—"greatly illuminated Warren's developing convictions about his craft at that crucial midpoint of his poetic career."[3] In subject matter and theme, the essays on Welty and Coleridge in particular forecast the treatment that Warren would give to the figure of Audubon more than two decades later.

In "Love and Separateness in Eudora Welty," Warren discusses at length Welty's short story "A Still Moment," in which the figure of Audubon plays a central role.[4] He observes "an irony of limit and contamination" in Audubon's relationship to his artistic subjects: "Let us take Audubon in relation to the heron. He loves the bird, innocently, in its fullness of being. But he must subject this love to knowledge; he must kill the bird if he is to commemorate its beauty, if he is to establish his communion with other men in terms of the bird's beauty" (*SE*, 162). This evaluation, especially in terms of Welty's theme of love and isolation, prefigures Warren's later treatment of Audubon. In a 1981 article tracing the source of *Audubon*, Max Webb comments that "facets of her [Welty's] richly imagined story recur in [Warren's] later poetic sequences so strongly that portions of her story . . . might serve as glosses to the 1969 poem."[5] The Audubon of Warren's poem, like the one in Welty's story, is a man "who can innocently accept nature," even as he is forced to recognize his inability to penetrate the membrane of nature's ideal unity.

Perhaps most significantly, Warren focuses on the theme of isolation, a subject he compares to the primary motif of *Rime of the Ancient Mariner:* "the story of a man who, having committed a crime, must try to re-establish his connection with humanity" (*SE*, 199). Warren's mention of the Mariner in conjunction with Welty's prevailing theme of isolation hints at another of Warren's projects at the

3. Warren, "An Interview with Robert Penn Warren," by Stitt, in *Talking with Robert Penn Warren*, ed. Watkins et al., 244, 333; Strandberg, *Poetic Vision*, 37.

4. The essay "Love and Separateness in Eudora Welty" is taken from *SE*, 156–69.

5. Max Webb, "*Audubon: A Vision*: Robert Penn Warren's Response to Eudora Welty's 'A Still Moment,' " *Mississippi Quarterly* 34, no. 4 (fall 1981): 445–55.

time, "A Poem of Pure Imagination." It would be difficult to reiterate the entire critical debate that has emerged since "A Poem of Pure Imagination" first appeared, but what is important to this discussion is the essay's pertinence to Warren's poetic development. Warren's criticism during the 1940s reveals the incubation of ideas that permeate his work. In *American Poets: From the Puritans to the Present*, Hyatt Waggoner comments that Warren's "steady progress toward the romantic, the direct, the personal, and the visionary" throughout his poetic career might startle anyone who considered him foremost and solely as a "contributor to *I'll Take My Stand* and co-author of the most influential New Critical textbook, *Understanding Poetry*." Strandberg attributes the beginnings of the second major phase of Warren's poetic career as well as the creative starting point of *Audubon* to a "conversion experience" that occurred in Warren's mental life during the mid-1940s. According to Strandberg, "this thrust derived from his [Warren's] reading of Romantic poets who themselves testified to experiencing cosmic consciousness, most notably Samuel Taylor Coleridge." The conclusion that Strandberg reaches about Warren's essay on Coleridge, that it "turns out to be an explanation and vindication of Warren's own purpose and practice in poetry," prefigures and reinforces Warren's own summation of *Audubon:* "And then in the end the poem is about Audubon and me."[6]

Warren's identification with the figure of Audubon in his poem signifies, as Ruppersburg suggests, "the poet's relationship to a historical and cultural past." *Audubon* could possibly be considered an exploration of intertwined accretions of myth, a "metamyth," since Audubon's own "official version of his identity" was a blend of legend bearing "a number of flattering embellishments" (*CP*, 253). Warren's associations not only with the Audubon who "walked in the world"

6. Waggoner, *American Poets*, 543–59. Although several Warren scholars have touched tentatively on the issue of Warren's Romanticism, Strandberg offers one of the most insightful explorations of the impact that Warren's study of the English Romantics had upon his developing craft; see *Poetic Vision*, 31. Warren's quote comes from the 1977 interview with Peter Stitt as reprinted in *Talking with Robert Penn Warren*, ed. Watkins et al., 244.

but also with the universal issues of knowledge and identity attest to his heightened sense of a "cosmic consciousness" (to use Strandberg's phrase)—the awareness of "the One Life within us and abroad / Which meets all motion and becomes its soul" (to use Coleridge's phrase). Among the figures of study Warren found most congenial to his own developing views, Coleridge probably had the greatest influence, although Warren's poetry (*Audubon* included) also indicates the influence of other Romantics such as Wordsworth, Shelley, and Keats. Yet the beginnings of Warren's Romantic vision originated in large part from his close study of Coleridge. Elements of Coleridgean Romanticism appear throughout *Audubon*, especially in Warren's creation of a figure who represents not only the "blessedness" of earned vision but also the isolation that comes with knowledge. *Audubon* presents a visionary blending of the Audubon of history and Warren's own imaginative appropriation of Audubon "as the poet's personal symbol of his struggles in the world, of creative passion."[7]

Throughout his career, Warren held a certain fascination for Coleridge, often citing the Romantic poet in relation to his own work. In a 1959 interview in which he was paired with Flannery O'Connor at the annual Vanderbilt Literary Symposium, Warren answered a question about the poetic process. His reply could just as easily have been applied to his own endeavors in writing the still-embryonic *Audubon*: "People have done it the other way, in cases: starting out with an idea, and hunting the fable, as they used to say. Coleridge is a good example of it. He says he had his theme for *The Ancient Mariner* for years. He kept casting around for the appropriate fable. He even made a false start or two, until he hit the right story. Those are not contradictory things, I think, because the theme was in him. He had at least reached some pretty clear intellectual definition of it before he started." In "A Poem of Pure Imagination," Warren examines not only Coleridge's primary themes but also the composition process, how Coleridge's "clear and burning Idea" evolved

7. Ruppersburg, *American Imagination*, 79; Strandberg, *Poetic Vision*, 31; Coleridge, "The Eolian Harp," in *Samuel Taylor Coleridge*, ed. Jackson, 28; Ruppersburg, *American Imagination*, 79.

into a fable about the poetic process. During his work on *Audubon*, Warren himself experienced "false starts." Like Coleridge, Warren stumbled in finding "the frame . . . , the narrative line."[8] Also like Coleridge, the "theme was in him," a theme similar to Welty's concept of the isolated naturalist who ironically must destroy what he loves in order to render it accessible to his imaginative vision.

That Coleridge had such a profound effect on Warren is clearly evident from the numerous variations of Mariner-like characters scattered throughout his writing—Willie Proudfit in *Night Rider*, Ashby Wyndham in *At Heaven's Gate*, Jack Burden in *All the King's Men*, Little Billie Potts in "The Ballad of Billie Potts," Hamish Bond in *Band of Angels*, and Blanding Cottshill in *Flood*, to name just a few. Justus sees the Mariner pattern emerging in a singular fashion that was interrelated with Warren's reading: "The primary narrative situation in Coleridge's poem is the overlay and constant impingement of two storytellers: the Mariner and the omniscient poet whose emotional alliance is with the Wedding Guest. What the Mariner tells his auditor is the substance of what the poet tells us, and in the telling he is forced to adopt the vision of the Mariner both to make moral sense of the experience and to retain the aesthetic power to galvanize quiescent and complacent souls to attention. That double concern is precisely Warren's."[9] The figure of the Mariner poses a striking antecedent for Warren's Audubon, particularly in the emphasis on "passion," a central concept in the Romantic tradition. Audubon's "expiation of guilt" pertains to his inner torments concerning his responsibilities as husband and social being as well as his fear of betraying his ideals and his vision of nature. Yet his "passion" compels him to remain true to his art. His quest for knowledge thus parallels the Romantic pattern exhibited in *Rime:* the realization of separateness, the journey toward redemption and regeneration, and the discovery

8. Flannery O'Connor and Robert Penn Warren, "An Interview with Flannery O'Connor and Robert Penn Warren," in *Talking with Robert Penn Warren*, ed. Watkins et al., 53; Coleridge quoted in *SE*, 209; Warren, "An Interview with Robert Penn Warren," *ibid.*, 244.

9. Justus, *Achievement*, 25.

of identity through achieving a "sacramental vision of the universe" (*SE*, 249).

Thus we are faced with the question of art and identity, two crucial issues for Warren as well as the Romantics. One of the most significant legacies of the Romantics was their belief that the imagination shaped the external world as well as the individual self, and Warren's essay on Coleridge reiterates this notion regarding both the internal "meaning" of the poem and the poet's creative process. Homer Obed Brown argues in "The Art of Theology and the Theology of Art" that while Warren accomplishes his goal of establishing the *Rime*'s organically formulated and intrinsic meaning, he also uses this essay as a vehicle "to make his own statement about the nature of poetry, of literary criticism, of life, and of the relationships between them."[10] The idea for a poem, Warren maintains, may ultimately be transformed by the imagination, but it must first be rooted in experience: "Actually, the creation of a poem is as much a process of discovery as a process of making. A poem may, in fact, start from an idea—and may involve any number of ideas—but the process for the poet is the process of discovering what the idea 'means' to him in the light of his total being and his total experience" (*SE*, 268). Here, as in *Audubon*, Warren links the artistic imagination with not only the discovery of an idea or subject but also with the process of exploring the undiscovered self.

The idea of the undiscovered self, one of the themes Warren finds central in Coleridge's poem, developed into an integral leitmotif in many of his later works. "Knowledge and the Image of Man," Warren's 1955 personal and artistic manifesto, elucidates the ideological processes he had been working through since the 1940s. The phrase he coins in this essay, the "osmosis of being" ("Knowledge," 185), has far-reaching implications for both his discussion of Coleridge and his subsequent poetry. Although an "osmosis of being" may appear to

10. Homer Obed Brown, "The Art of Theology and the Theology of Art: Robert Penn Warren's Reading of Coleridge's *The Rime of the Ancient Mariner*," *Boundary: A Journal of Postmodern Literature and Culture* 8, no. 1 (fall 1979): 239.

imply a negation of individual personality or a complete absorption
into the "One Life within us and abroad," Warren firmly emphasizes
that this "osmosis" involves experience on the most personal and subjective level: "[Man] is, rather, in the world with continual and intimate interpenetration, an inevitable osmosis of being, which in the
end does not deny, but affirms, his identity" ("Knowledge," 185). The
moment of crisis and vision ultimately leads to the realization of
the "primal sympathy" between human beings and nature as well as
individual identity, a concept Coleridge as well as Wordsworth and
other Romantic contemporaries address.

The issue of identity lies at the center of *Audubon*. Ruppersburg
asserts that Audubon's identity is "rooted in passionate involvement
with nature (and, by implication, estrangement from humanity)."
Seen in this light, both the Mariner and Audubon embody what
Frank Kermode refers to as "the artist in isolation." In *Romantic
Image*, Kermode examines two beliefs central to the Romantic tradition, "the Image as a radiant truth out of space and time, and . . . the
necessary isolation or estrangement of men who can perceive it."[11]
The Mariner's "art" becomes his "passion," which implies both suffering and glory. Warren reads *The Rime of the Ancient Mariner* as
Coleridge's exploration of poetic practice and individual identity, and
Audubon functions in the same way for Warren. Audubon, the man
who must "walk in the world," parallels the poet in "American Portrait: Old Style," who realizes that "I love the world even in my
anger / And that's a hard thing to outgrow" (*CP*, 342). The ability to
"love the world," to offer a blessing in spite of the burden of experience, aligns Warren with his Romantic predecessors, who stressed
the subjective power of the individual mind. Yet the internalized passion of the artist, for the Romantics as well as for Warren, does not
entail solipsistic aversion to the human condition but awakens him to
"a deep engagement of spirit with the world" ("Knowledge," 188).

Coleridge's Mariner and Warren's Audubon are indeed estranged
from humanity by their passion, but it is significant that while they

11. Ruppersburg, *American Imagination*, 82; Frank Kermode, *Romantic
Image* (London: Routledge and Kegan Paul, 1957), 2.

suffer the isolation associated with this passion, their ultimate motion is toward humanity. As the creator of the Audubon we encounter in the poem, Warren presents the imagination in its power to "provide the great discipline of sympathy" (*SE*, 255). Such an affirmation of the imagination is, according to Abrams, the essence of the Romantic aesthetic. As Coleridge said, poetry, like all art, "is purely human; for all its materials are from the mind, and all its products are for the mind."[12] Similarly, near the end of the section entitled "Love and Knowledge," we see the final manifestation of Audubon's passion for painting birds: "He put them where they are, and there we see them: / In our imagination" (*CP*, 266).

Audubon's paintings of birds, however, are not the focus of the poem. Rather, Warren emphasizes the passion that breeds art. Audubon's passion sets him apart from other men, and like the Mariner, this passion results in the projection or assertion of selfhood. His search for identity is inextricably linked to his "passion": "what / Is man but his passion?" (*CP*, 254). In his reading of the *Rime*, Warren connects the Mariner's predicament with the plight of the artist, drawing parallels between the Mariner's compulsive recitation of his story and the role of the artist in a world indifferent to creative endeavors or inspirations. Warren finds that "in the end of the poem we have another fable of the creative process, and perhaps a fuller statement of Coleridge's conception of the poet, the man with the power which comes unbidden and which is an 'agony' until it finds words, the power which wells up from the unconscious but which is the result of a moral experience and in its product, the poem, the 'tale' told by the Mariner, will 'teach'—for that is the word the Mariner uses" (*SE*, 258). Paradoxically, the Mariner is isolated from humanity because of the "sacramental vision" he has achieved, yet he must "teach" others about the nature of his revelation. In his comments on Welty's story, Warren argues that Audubon's isolation is the result of his artistic passion: "Here, too, the fact of the isolation is realized: as artist and lover of nature he has aspired to a communication, a commu-

12. Coleridge quoted in Abrams, *Natural Supernaturalism*, 429.

nion, with other men in terms of the bird, but now 'he saw his long labor most revealingly at the point where it met its limit' and he is forced back upon himself" (*SE*, 162). Similarly, the Mariner is an isolated figure who has achieved "knowledge" by shooting the albatross, although at a painful cost. Welty's Audubon, and later Warren's, also gains knowledge by killing birds, and the price of this knowledge is his isolation, his "set-apartness" from the rest of humanity.

Yet as the opening section, "Was Not the Lost Dauphin," reveals, this passion does not necessarily entail a complete merger with nature. When Audubon "leans on his gun. Thinks / How thin is the membrane between himself and world" (*CP*, 255), we become aware that there is a barrier and that Warren does not intend to propose that art dissolves the breach between man and nature. When Audubon is "forced back upon himself" (*SE*, 162) because of the impermeability of the "membrane," he must return to the world of mortality and decay. The idyllic world of nature offers scenes of "the bear, / Daft in the honey-light" and the bee whose "wings, like mica, glint / In the sunlight" (*CP*, 254–55), like Keats's imagined supernal realm of the nightingale, but Audubon cannot be *of* this world; it is Other, a distinction realized by Warren's Romantic predecessors. Art may not heal the breach between man and nature, but as the Romantics and Warren propose, creative vision is a means, not an end, and in the process it may lead man toward a fuller understanding of himself and his role in the world.

Although *Audubon* in many ways presents an affirmative vision of the poetic and artistic imagination, Warren, like his Romantic predecessors, suggests that the vision will not come cheaply. The necessary estrangement in itself creates a gulf between the artist and society. The Mariner approaches the festive wedding party, yet he appears freakish and strange to his somewhat reluctant listener. In the end, the Mariner must "pass, like night, from land to land," searching for peace from his isolation, his "agony."[13] Likewise, in section V of the poem, "The Sound of That Wind," Audubon "walked in the world"

13. Coleridge, *The Rime of the Ancient Mariner*, in *Samuel Taylor Coleridge*, ed. Jackson, 64.

and "Knew the lust of the eye," but his passion separates him from the rest of society, leaving him to "dangle . . . In the lobbies and couloirs of greatness" (CP, 264).

The gravest danger of "walking in the world," however, lies in the necessary encounters with forces far removed from nature's ideal realm—forces that, in the end, reaffirm the "osmosis of being" and the complicity of human experience. The second and longest section of *Audubon*, "The Dream He Never Knew the End Of," presents a nightmare world that stands in stark contrast to the scenes in "Was Not the Lost Dauphin":

> Shank-end of day, spit of snow, the call,
> A crow, sweet in distance, then sudden
> The clearing: among stumps, ruined cornstalks yet standing, the spot
> Like a wound rubbed raw in the vast pelt of the forest. There
> Is the cabin, a huddle of logs with no calculation or craft:
> The human filth, the human hope.
>
> (CP, 255)

"Lean[ing] on his gun" (CP, 255) Audubon contemplates this scene as he does the bear in the preceding section, but the cabin does not evoke the same sense of reverie. If anything, the "membrane between himself and the world" seems cloudier and far more impenetrable than before. Audubon stays at the cabin for the night, by degrees becoming aware that the woman who lives there and her three sons plan to murder him in his sleep. However, three travelers burst into the cabin before the woman and her sons can carry out their plans to kill him (supposedly, for his gold watch).

Warren imaginatively transforms this episode in a way that places historical fact within the realm of myth. The "infernal hag" that Audubon describes in the actual episode from the *Ornithological Biography* becomes a wilderness "Night-mare Life-in-Death" similar in many ways to the demon woman who gambles for the Mariner's soul in Coleridge's poem.[14] While Audubon's confrontation with the "In-

14. *Ibid.*, 52.

fernal hag" is not the direct result of any crime against nature (as is the case with the Mariner), it is an integral part of his initiation into the dark realities of human experience. If *Audubon* is, as Warren writes about the *Rime*, a tale of "reconciliation" (*SE*, 214) then the woman in the cabin acts as the agent of reconciliation. Audubon's initial reaction to her is one of revulsion, and Warren portrays her as witchlike:

> The face, in the air, hangs. Large,
> Raw-hewn, strong-beaked, the haired mole
> Near the nose, to the left, and the left side by firelight
> Glazed red, the right in shadow, and under the tumble and tangle
> Of dark hair on that head, and under the coarse eyebrows,
> The eyes, dark, glint as from the unspecifiable
> Darkness of a cave. It is a woman.
>
> (*CP*, 256)

What the historical Audubon recounts as a close brush with death, Warren shapes into a central moment of epiphany. The woman, though crude and witchlike, arouses in Audubon an awareness not only of her femaleness but also of her humanity. Her face becomes "sweet in an outrage of sweetness, so that / His guts twist cold. He cannot bear what he sees" (*CP*, 256). The woman represents the opposite of the ideal Audubon is seeking in the wilderness, even, as Ruppersburg and Bedient point out, the opposite of Lucy, the wife he has left behind in order to pursue his art.[15]

If poetry does, as Warren asserts in "Knowledge and the Image of Man," reconcile "the ugly with the beautiful" ("Knowledge," 188), then Wordsworth's "spot of time" performs that function for Audubon. At first, the hag in the cabin fills Audubon with a sense of revulsion, and he cannot reconcile this vision of humanity in its basest form to either his ideal world of nature or of idealized womanhood.

---

15. Ruppersburg, *American Imagination*, 86; Bedient, *In the Heart's Last Kingdom*, 142–43.

Yet she entrances him, compelling him by degrees to recognize the "new dimension of beauty" (*CP*, 260) she represents, especially in death. If we consider the poem (and this section in particular) in conjunction with Warren's reading of Coleridge, then the woman in the cabin provides the same catalyst toward "blessedness" as the sea snakes in the *Rime*. The Mariner curses the sea snakes at first—"a thousand thousand slimy things / Lived on"—yet his eventual blessing of these same creatures leads toward his redemption: "A spring of love gushed from my heart, / And I blessed them unaware."[16]

In Warren's analysis, the blessing the Mariner bestows upon the sea snakes regenerates him into the "One Life"; he regains "the state of 'immanence' in wisdom and love" (*SE*, 232–33). By acknowledging his connection to the "despise[d] creature of the calm," the Mariner's initial curse is broken, allowing him to be incorporated back into the "sympathy which binds human society" (*SE*, 255). To use the phrase from "Knowledge and the Image of Man" that parallels Coleridge's concept of the "One Life," the "osmosis of being" that Audubon achieves in "The Dream He Never Knew the End Of" is also determined by a despised "Other." In the moment of the woman's death, her ugliness transforms into beauty at Audubon's realization that despite the baseness and dreariness of the woman's life, there is something fierce and determined, an aggressive and conscious acceptance of death, in the way she approaches her execution.

Warren's variation on what Frank Kermode calls "the Romantic Moment," when *chronos* suddenly becomes *kairos*, takes an object (or in this case, an objectified human being) out of its context in the ordinary world and places it within an arrested moment. The function of the "moment," according to M. H. Abrams, is to illuminate the "charismatic revelation in the commonplace or trivial object." Abrams traces the development of the modern equivalent of the "Romantic Moment" from Wordsworth's "spots of time" to Faulkner's "instant of sublimation . . . a flash, a glare," and Warren himself cred-

16. William Wordsworth, *The Prelude*, ed. Jonathan Wordsworth, M. H. Abrams, and Stephen Gill (New York: Norton, 1979); 428; Coleridge, *A Critical Edition of the Major Works*, ed. Jackson.

ited Faulkner with using "the image of a frieze for such a moment of frozen action."[17] Warren also admired Welty's treatment of the moment of heightened consciousness that comes unbidden in "A Still Moment." Although he and Welty present different events leading to Audubon's epiphany, both moments represent what Warren calls "the discovery of the two poles—the dream and the world; the idea and nature; innocence and experience; individuality and the anonymous, devouring life-flux; meaning and force; love and knowledge" (*SE*, 163).

The epiphany of Warren's Audubon, however, does not signal a resolution. Audubon's moment of insight, while physically ("So becomes aware that he is in the manly state") (*CP*, 259) and emotionally stimulating, leads him only toward further questions:

> He thinks: "What has been denied me?"
> Thinks: "There is never an answer."
> Thinks: "The question is the only answer."
>
> (*CP*, 260)

This inability to achieve ultimate discovery or resolution does not lessen the impact of the moment. Central to Romantic philosophy was the belief that all of human experience is constituted by successive "moments" of sensation in consciousness. Wordsworth's *Prelude* does not end with his epiphany on Snowdon, and each "spot of time" that he encounters marks but one realization in a series of moments.[18] Audubon "yearns to be able to frame a definition of joy" (*CP*, 260) after his encounter at the cabin, but the next section of the poem, entitled "We Are Only Ourselves" (the shortest segment of the entire work), emphasizes the necessity of perseverance:

17. Frank Kermode, *The Sense of an Ending* (London: Routledge and Kegan Paul, 1967), 47; Abrams, *Natural Supernaturalism*, 421, 419; Warren, "Warren on the Art of Fiction," interview by Ellison and Walter, in *Talking with Robert Penn Warren*, ed. Watkins et al., 39.

18. Wordsworth, *The Prelude*, ed. Wordsworth et al., 428.

We never know what we have lost, or what we have found.
We are only ourselves, and that promise.
Continue to walk in the world. Yes, love it!
He continued to walk in the world.

(CP, 261)

For Warren as well as his Romantic forerunners, the artist's link with nature extends to his link with other men. Although the artist and nature cannot merge completely, there is still the "promise" of renewed vision that comes with each successive moment of revelation. To "walk in the world" is to recognize both the joy and the limitation of human existence.

Audubon's passion enables him to "walk in the world," despite his discovery that he cannot transcend his human self. As Warren notes in his discussion of "A Still Moment," Audubon is ultimately "forced back upon himself" (*SE*, 162). The Romantics realized that even after moments of transcendent vision the individual inevitably must return to his mortal, earthbound self, but these moments are a part of the process of self-definition. Joy therefore becomes possible not *despite* human limitations but *because* of them. Yet for Warren as well as for the Romantics, an awareness of limitation does not suppress the longing for an ideal sense of selfhood. In the fourth section of *Audubon*, "The Sign Whereby He Knew," the speaker poignantly voices Audubon's (and his own) desire for identity:

To wake in some dawn and see,
As though down a rifle barrel, lined up
Like sights, the self that was, the self that is, and there,
Far off but in range, completing that alignment, your fate.

(CP, 261)

The hunting metaphor used here is doubly appropriate: Audubon literally has to shoot birds in order to paint them, but he also envisions his art as a projection of selfhood, his means of attempting merger with the ideal. Each moment of epiphany leads Audubon toward self-definition, but the "blessedness!" of such exactitude, however, is impossible chiefly because it *is* outside the limits of human existence and belongs to the unattainable: "This is not a dimension of Time"(*CP*, 261).

Time is what Audubon is forced to live in, despite his attempts to submerge himself in nature, apart from the dull reality of social responsibility. Part B of "The Sign Whereby He Knew" begins with the ideal realm of nature responding to the cycles of time ("In this season the waters shrink"), yet it is part of a timelessness in which Audubon cannot participate (". . . nothing disturbs the infinite blue of the sky") (*CP*, 262). It is not nature that is altered by time but the vision of the observer that changes, as Wordsworth lamented in both "Tintern Abbey" and in the *Intimations Ode*. The child in both poems takes part in a form of Platonic unity with nature, unaware of division between self and nature. The "glad animal movements" of childhood temporarily unite the child and nature in a lack of self-awareness.[19] (In "The Flower," one of the Rosanna poems in *Promises*, Warren's daughter can "sing as though human need / Were not for perfection" [*CP*, 106].) But Audubon is an adult who must "walk in the world" (*CP*, 261) and therefore experience the inevitable division that time and knowledge bring. In "Knowledge and the Image of Man," Warren writes of the process of self-definition: "[Man's] unity with nature will not now be that of a drop of water in the ocean; it is, rather, the unity of the lover with the beloved, a unity presupposing separateness" (186). Although Audubon is in nature and is himself a part of nature, that he is human and therefore must seek self-definition sets him apart from other creatures, such as the tusked boar who "grumble[s] in his ivy slick" (*CP*, 262) and the jay, natural elements who can simply exist. Self-consciousness creates the division between humans and nature. This is part of the membrane's impermeability.

The vision of nature that Warren evokes throughout many of the poems in *Promises* appears in *Audubon*, again reinforcing the realiza-

---

19. Wordsworth, "Lines Composed a Few Miles above Tintern Abbey," in *Selected Poems and Prefaces*, ed. Stillinger, 109.

tion that he reaches in "Court-martial": "The world is real. It is
there" (*CP*, 113). As Warren writes in *Audubon*,

> The world declares itself. That voice
> Is vaulted in—oh, arch on arch—redundancy of joy, its end
> Is its beginning, necessity
> Blooms like a rose.
>
> (*CP*, 263)

Yet although "The world declares itself," the truth found in nature is
inexpressible: "Why, / Therefore, is truth the only thing that cannot /
Be spoken?" (*CP*, 263). "Truth" cannot be spoken because language,
like the "membrane" that separates humans from nature, frustrates
any attempts to attain the merger that Audubon seeks. This inability
to attain his ideal, however, does not prevent him from pursuing
meaning and identity. Rather, as the opening lines of "The Sign
Whereby He Knew" imply, his acceptance of what his life was, "as
he was / In the end" (*CP*, 261), indicates the Wordsworthian consolation of the "Strength in what remains behind." That acceptance is
what makes Warren's vision of Audubon a celebration of one man's
passion and his fidelity to his art.

"The Sound of That Wind," the fifth section of the poem, stands
out as the most evocative juxtaposition of the historical Audubon's
journals and Warren's imaginative reconstructions of them. In a passage from *Ornithological Biography*, which Warren includes in this
section, Audubon proudly notes his refusal to accept the "promise of
ease" and "the kind condescension of Daniel Webster": ". . . 'would
give me a fat place was I willing to / have one; but I love indepenn
and piece more / than humbug and money'" (*CP*, 264). In *The Mirror and the Lamp*, Abrams describes Keats in a way that equally pertains to Audubon: both exhibit "that peculiarly modern malady—a
conscious and persistent conflict between the requirements of social
responsibility and of aesthetic detachment."[20] Structurally, "The

20. Abrams, *Mirror and the Lamp*, 328.

Sound of That Wind" reinforces the conflicts between Audubon's sense of responsibility to convention and his fidelity to artistic perception. As in "The Sign Whereby He Knew," Warren returns in "The Sound of That Wind" to the notion that Audubon could have easily succumbed to the temptations of a "normal" life—"Keep store, dandle babies, and at night nuzzle / The hazelnut-shaped sweet tits of Lucy, and / With the piratical mark-up of the frontier, get rich"— and avoided the world's estimation of him as "being of weak character" (*CP*, 262). In the most reductive analysis, Audubon's life could very well be seen as a failure: he refuses the complacencies of wealth and domestic security, and he spends most of his life seeking an unattainable merger between self and nature. Yet he remains true to his "passion" (*CP*, 254), exhibiting a fidelity to imaginative vision that Warren praises throughout his portrait of Audubon. As the poet's artistic creation, Audubon is transformed into a symbolic figure of inspiration and the power of the imagination.

While the interspersed entries from Audubon's journals serve to reinforce the naturalist's place within history (and therefore, time), Part B of "The Sound of That Wind" transports us out of Audubon's time into the present: "So died in his bed, and / Night leaned, and now leans, / Off the Atlantic, and is on schedule" (*CP*, 265). Night, or death, is a universal constant, and just as Audubon's "mind / Was darkened" (*CP*, 264) by the finitude of the human life cycle, so too must other elements of nature succumb to time. The merciless motion of time unifies all things—Audubon, "the shack of a sheepherder, high above the Bitterroot," and "The Northwest Orient plane, New York to Seattle" (*CP*, 265)—yet this unity does not preclude an overwhelming sense of isolation and distance. These images of the uncompromising continuation of time suggest a universe devoid of meaning in and of itself. The quotation from Ecclesiastes that opens Part C of "The Sound of That Wind" ("For everything there is a season") seems to intensify the sense of man's necessary submission to undeviating patterns of nature. "But," Warren adds, "there is the dream / Of a season past all seasons" (*CP*, 265). The "dream" signifies the fusion of memory and imagination, like Wordsworth's "spots of time" in which an ordinary event takes on particular meaning by virtue of the imagination. Time is suspended in this moment, allowing only the briefest glimpse of possible transcendence. The timeless "dream" in "The Sound of That Wind" represents an ideal, like Audubon's desire for complete unity with nature, that cannot exist in time; such a world can only live in the imagination.

Warren's vision of the timeless dream also evokes images from Keats's poetry, especially the imagined "vintage" in "Ode to a Nightingale," the "beaker full of the warm South," which can transport the poet beyond the world "Where youth grows pale, and spectre-thin, and dies."[21] In Part C of "The Sound of That Wind," time is paradoxically suspended yet fluid: "In such a dream the wild-grape cluster, / High-hung, exposed in the gold light, / Unripening, ripens" (CP, 265). Another person in the vision, possibly a loved one, has tasted these grapes: "Stained, the lip with wetness gleams." In the stasis of memory, where the imagination is not subject to time, the lip remains "undrying . . . in the bright wind," although the speaker "cannot hear the sound of that wind" (CP, 265). The wind, like the symbolic image of night in Part B, denotes the passage of time, but as Warren writes earlier in "The Sign Whereby He Knew," the realm of the imagination, of the ideal, "is not a dimension of Time" (CP, 261). Thus this intensely personal fragment encapsulates the entire "vision" of the poet itself, broadening Audubon's passion into every individual's search for wholeness and identity.

The next section, "Love and Knowledge," returns to Audubon, but here Warren has entirely transplanted the Audubon of history. Again, we are reminded of the concrete source of Audubon's art through the lyrical descriptions of the birds he paints:

> Their footless dance
> Is of the beautiful liability of their nature.
> Their eyes are round, boldly convex, bright as a jewel,
> And merciless . . .

21. John Keats, "Ode to a Nightingale," in *Selected Poems*, ed. Barnard, 169–70.

> . . . They fly
> In air that glitters like fluent crystal
> And is hard as perfectly transparent iron, they cleave it
> With no effort.
>
> (*CP*, 266)

Despite their inherent beauty, they are still separate, still Other. In and of themselves, the birds yield no meaning except that which the imagination bestows. Audubon aspires to "know" the birds that inspire his passion, and killing them is the only way he can "know" them.[22] To paraphrase Wordsworth in "The Tables Turned," Audubon murders to dissect, kills to understand. In his discussion of "A Still Moment," Warren explains, "But having killed the bird, [Audubon] knows that the best he can make of it now in a painting would be a dead thing, 'never the essence, only a sum of parts,' and that 'it would always meet with a stranger's sight, and never be one with the beauty in any other man's head in the world' " (*SE*, 162). Although the image becomes eternal through art, the passion of the artist must be relegated to a "Cold Pastoral," static and lifeless.[23] Paradoxically, Audubon's creative act involves the death of his subjects. Although definition brings loss, the loss is a necessary constituent not only of art but also of life. The final statement at the end of "Love and Knowledge" recaptures the complexity of the passion that engenders art and identity: "What is love? / One name for it is knowledge" (*CP*, 266).

The concluding section of *Audubon*, "Tell Me a Story," abandons the figure of Audubon completely, turning instead to the poet's own

22. Audubon's birds, according to Warren's "vision" of how Audubon perceives his subjects, become images but not "pure" images. As Roland Barthes explains in "Rhetoric of the Image" (in *Classic Essays on Photography*, ed. Alan Trachtenberg [New Haven: Leete's Island Books, 1980], 269), "The image is representation, which is to say ultimately resurrection, and, as we know, the intelligible is reputed antipathetic to lived experience."

23. John Keats, "Ode on a Grecian Urn," in *Selected Poems*, ed. Barnard, 169.

"collocation / Of memories" (*CP*, 108) (a phrase from the poem "Colder Fire" in *Promises*). Like many of the poems in *Promises*, "Tell Me a Story" shifts to the poet's recollections of childhood, the "landscape lost in the heart's homely deep" (*CP*, 131). As Ruppersburg explains, "The concluding poem contrasts the promise of the past with the despair and need of the present day." The need for "promises" takes on special urgency "In this century, and moment, of mania," (*CP*, 267), and the poet summons a memory of a more innocent time, at least within his own life, to combat the cynicism of his mature experience. Like the poetic sequence in *Promises* entitled "Boy's Will, Joyful Labor without Pay, and Harvest Home (1918)," Warren imaginatively recreates his own "spot of time" out of memory:

> Long ago, in Kentucky, I, a boy, stood
> By a dirt road, in first dark, and heard
> The great geese hoot northward.
> I could not see them, there being no moon
> And the stars sparse. I heard them.
> I did not know what was happening in my heart.
>
> (*CP*, 266)

Like many of Wordsworth's epiphanal moments in *The Prelude* (in Book Second, Wordsworth recalls hearing "an invisible bird" singing "so sweetly 'mid the gloom" that he wishes to "have lived forever there / To hear such music") or Keats's poetic response to the unseen nightingale, such a moment of awareness creates a longing for an ideal world.[24]

The world itself, however, is not the ideal, especially not in the present time of the poem. Critics such as William Bedford Clark, Justus, and Ruppersburg note the significance of the poem's publication date—1969—and although the idea for Audubon originated in the 1940s (a turbulent enough time in itself), Warren drafted "Tell

---

24. Ruppersburg, *American Imagination*, 100; Wordsworth, *The Prelude*, ed. Wordsworth et al., 72.

Me a Story" in January of 1969.[25] Ruppersburg suggests that the tragic events of the 1960s, and 1968 in particular, must have "convinced [Warren] that his own time can offer no source of wonder to provoke and enlarge the imagination," and certainly the "mania" of his "century, and moment" called for a restoration of ideals to combat the period's disillusionment.[26] Thus, at the conclusion of the poem, the poet expresses the need for a "story of deep delight" (*CP*, 267). This yearning for a renewed sense of wonder, like the passion that compels Audubon in his search for meaning, connects the past with the present, the "visionary gleam" of childhood with the adult's attempts to regain that vision. Yet as Warren and the Romantics realized, the original unity of the past cannot be resurrected in its entirety. The redemptive power of the imagination works in arrests of time, but since "The name of the story will be Time," the poet tells us, "you must not pronounce its name" (*CP*, 267). The ideal world of the past cannot be literally reconstructed. It can only be envisioned through the imagination and memory. Time's "name" cannot be pronounced because it is the agent that separates the past from the present. The "story" must be about "Time" but outside of time as well, the "timeless moment" that constitutes our awareness of self within a continuity. The story must be one of "deep delight," as the last line of the poem reinforces. This line restates the poet's longing to be told "a story of deep delight" (*CP*, 267), because only through the imagination can the distance time brings be suspended.

Such is the nature of Warren's vision of Audubon. The poet's "story" transforms the American ornithologist into a figure representing inspiration and artistic passion, particularly for Warren. The

---

25. Anthony Szczesiul's "Robert Penn Warren's *Audubon*: Vision and Rvision" (*Mississippi Quarterly* 47, no. 1 [winter 1993–94]: 3–14) gives one of the most detailed accounts of the textual history of *Audubon*, drawing on the holograph drafts of the poem from Warren's papers in the Beinecke Rare Book and Manuscript Library at Yale University. For discussion concerning the thematic relevance of the poem's publication date, see Ruppersburg, *American Imagination*, 101.

26. Ruppersburg, *American Imagination*, 101.

structure of the poem becomes a series of timeless moments in the way that Warren envisions the historical Audubon, each fragmentary piece of Audubon's (and Warren's) experience coming together to form a larger totality. Even the creative process that resulted in *Audubon* can be seen as a succession of epiphanies for Warren. He told Richard B. Sale in a 1969 interview that he "had been working on [*Audubon*] for many, many months, started it twenty years ago. But then this section came in a flash . . . and I knew exactly what the poem was going to be, what I was shooting for." Warren later repeated this account to Peter Stitt in 1977, explaining that after setting the poem aside for more than twenty years, one morning (while making the bed) he recalled the first line of his original attempt, and "suddenly saw" how to proceed with the poem's narrative structure: "I did it in fragments, sort of snapshots of Audubon."[27] The idea of "fragments" or "snapshots" of Audubon reinforces Welty's use of the "still moment" in her short story by the same title. In a larger sense, it also captures the essence of the Romantic moment, the arrest of time in which insight or heightened consciousness appears suddenly, as transitory as it is unpremeditated.

With so many sources converging toward the making of *Audubon*, it is not surprising that Warren labored with his initial conception of the poem for more than two decades. In "A Poem of Pure Imagination," Warren almost self-prophetically claims, "In the case of *The Ancient Mariner* we have good evidence that the poet was working in terms of a preconceived theme, and we know that the original composition required some months and that the process of revision required years" (*SE*, 269). The figure of Audubon that emerges in Warren's poem is another Mariner, alone in nature, albeit a distinctly American individualist on the edge of a diminishing frontier. Yet the issues of the imagination, artistic passion, and identity at the core of the poem transcend the historical Audubon, making him the em-

27. Robert Penn Warren, "An Interview in New Haven with Robert Penn Warren," interview by Sale, in *Talking with Robert Penn Warren*, ed. Watkins et al., 119; Warren, "An Interview with Robert Penn Warren," by Stitt, *ibid.*, 244.

bodiment of the poet's personal search for meaning. Audubon's "passion," not his precise and detached paintings of birds, is what captivates Warren, aligning him with the Romantics in their belief in the "modifying action of passion." In a sense, the Audubon that Warren creates is a composite of several Romantic archetypes. He is the wanderer of Coleridge's *Rime*, who, as Warren describes in "A Poem of Pure Imagination," discovers the "One Life" and the "sacramental vision of the universe" (*SE*, 266) through his suffering and isolation. He is the fallen persona of Wordsworth's lyrics who seeks regeneration into the primal unity of nature. He is the solitary figure of Keats's poetry who desires merger with the Ideal. Even the title, *Audubon: A Vision*, suggests Blake's emphasis on the transformative power of the imagination. *Audubon* thus manifests Warren's most fully realized Romantic vision, and his poetic creation testifies to the power of the human spirit and imagination. Consider this statement from Wordsworth's Preface to *Lyrical Ballads* (1800): "Poetry is first and last of all knowledge—it is immortal as the heart of man."[28] Knowledge, as well as love, is the driving force behind Warren's *Audubon*.

28. Abrams, *Mirror and the Lamp*, 55; Wordsworth, Preface to the Second Edition of *Lyrical Ballads*, in *Selected Poems and Prefaces*, ed. Stillinger, 456.

V

Poetry, 1970–1985

In a series of interviews conducted in 1981, Robert Penn Warren explained to David Farrell what poetry had meant to him throughout his fifty-eight years of writing: "I would say poetry is a way of life, ultimately. . . . It's a way of being open to the world, a way of being open to experience. . . . I would also say that poetry is not like a profession, but a way of life. These are two quite different things."[1] If poetry had been merely a "profession" for Warren, he might easily have settled into the kind of retirement that most people anticipate after a lifetime of work. By the time *Audubon* was published, he had achieved a level of critical acclaim that ranked him among the best American writers of his time. He had won Pulitzer Prizes for both fiction and poetry, plus numerous other awards and honors. But instead of resting on his rather substantial laurels, Warren continued his persistent exploration of identity, truth, and time. The stance, style, and themes of his "late phase" of poetry attest to his continuous search for meaning, a search that increasingly progressed into the realm of the personal and the visionary. This subjective and visionary

1. Robert Penn Warren, "Poetry as a Way of Life: An Interview with Robert Penn Warren," interview by David Farrell, in *Talking with Robert Penn Warren*, ed. Watkins et al., 370.

quality, muted in his early poetry by traces of naturalistic despair, develops from *Promises* onward into a form of Romanticism that takes its power from Warren's observations and discoveries about human experience as well as his conviction that poetry was one of the most vital ways of exploring the self and its relationship to the human community. *Audubon* may represent a critical high point in Warren's poetic career, but as his poetry from 1969 until the end of his career reveals, the voice that asks in *Audubon*, "what / Is man but his passion?" (*CP*, 254) was not finished with the world yet.

Citing other great artists whose talents bloomed as they grew older, Hilton Kramer likens Warren's "late phase" to that of Beethoven, Verdi, Turner, Cézanne, and Matisse: "There is almost nothing more interesting—or more mysterious—in the annals of the artistic imagination than the phenomenon of the transcendent 'late' style that is achieved by certain creative minds in a final, protracted flowering of their talents and ambitions." We can expand Kramer's list to include William Butler Yeats, who, like Warren, developed his own brand of Romanticism and throughout his career linked himself to Romantic forerunners in his prose and poetry. Both poets, one standing at the dawn of Modernism and the other beginning his career at its height, created new Romantic modes that explored the issues and concerns of modern culture. While Warren may have begun writing poetry primarily under the influence of Eliot, his mature poetry, especially in the last two decades of his prolific output, more closely resembles Yeats's work in attitude and theme. Late in life, Yeats called himself "the last Romantic," but there was another Romantic voice yet to come. In his own distinctive manner, Warren continued the legacy of the nineteenth-century Romantics. As Paul Mariani writes, "Coming late in the Romantic tradition, Warren sees himself as a poet singing at evening," offering his own version of the Romantic sublime for the second half of the twentieth century.[2]

---

2. Hilton Kramer, "Robert Penn Warren and His Poetry," in *Homage to Robert Penn Warren: A Collection of Critical Essays*, ed. Frank Graziano (Durango, Colo.: Logbridge-Rhodes, 1981), 9. See also Paul Mariani, "Robert Penn Warren," in *Modern Critical Views: Robert Penn Warren*, ed. Harold Bloom (New York: Chelsea House Publishers, 1986), 223.

Like the Romantics, Warren emphasizes the unified indivisibility of moral action, individual as well as communal responsibility, and the need for an understanding of the past in order to discover a meaningful relationship with the present. Throughout his career he also asserts his belief that the poetic act was vital for both the individual and the culture at large. Shelley wrote that poetry "brings the whole soul of man into being."[3] Warren echoes this sentiment in *Democracy and Poetry:* "Poetry, even in the same act and the same moment, helps one to grasp reality and to grasp one's own life" (*DP*, 92). Warren immediately cautions, "Not that it will give definition and certainties," but he adds a statement of his belief about the nature and purpose of life: "I suppose I see life, for all our yearning for and struggle toward primal or supernal unity of being, as a more or less oscillating process" (*DP*, 93). Throughout the last two decades of his career, his work reveals the "oscillating process" that he explored in his own life. We often encounter Warren the skeptic, who, like Yeats, denounces in apocalyptic tones a modern society seemingly bent on its own destruction. *Democracy and Poetry* and "New Dawn," Warren's poem about the nuclear devastation of Hiroshima, ring with dire warnings of the dangers inherent in a technologically centered culture and the subsequent erosion of individual identity and communal values. In the nineteenth century, the Romantics had expressed alarm over the widespread shift to an industrialized society. In the twentieth century, Warren grimly evaluates the exploitation of scientific power in his own culture, with the effects ranging from individual solipsism to nuclear annihilation. As a result, Warren argues, the self becomes "maimed" in a modern society: "We lose contact with the world's body, lose any holistic sense of our relation to the world" (*DP*, 72). Often, in later poems such as *Audubon* and *Chief Joseph of the Nez Perce*, Warren turns to the historical past in his search for a "holistic sense" of meaning. In the process of evaluating the past, he also engages in a highly personal quest to construct meaning out of his own past and experience.

3. Shelley, "A Defence of Poetry," in *Shelley's Poetry and Prose*, ed. Reiman and Powers, 508.

As Warren so forcefully asserts in *Audubon*, self-definition comes from an acceptance of the world's inclusiveness, "the human filth, the human hope" (*CP*, 255) out of which arise the possibilities for joy. Nature increasingly provides the backdrop against which he places his observations about the human condition, often leaving the impression that some ineluctable *something* lies just beyond the grasp of mortal understanding. From the early poem "The Return: An Elegy" (1935) to "Time as Hypnosis" in *Or Else* (1974), Warren persistently asks for the "name of the world." Yet the "membrane" between self and nature, the ideal and the real, cannot be breached, a realization that he makes abundantly clear in *Audubon*. Whatever meaning can be taken from nature must be imperfectly filtered through human consciousness. In his final years of writing poetry, Warren relies heavily on memory and imagination as sources of inspiration. But his late poetry is not a lamentation for lost youth, nor is it a catalog of nostalgic reminiscences. If anything, his last works stress the idea of continuity: of history, of influence, of time and the world. Warren draws on what Wordsworth called "the strength in what remains behind" as the directive and impulse for his mature visions of communal "heart-joy" (*CP*, 104).[4]

The theme of continuity in the face of individual mortality unites the poems in *Or Else*, the collection published following *Audubon*, as well as the poems in *Can I See Arcturus From Where I Stand* (1976), *Now and Then* (1978), *Being Here* (1980), and *Rumor Verified* (1981). Warren was in his seventies when he wrote the poems in these volumes, and as he repeatedly returns to the "landscape lost in the heart's homely deep" (*CP*, 131), his search for a way to live takes on increasing urgency. In poems from *Or Else*, such as "I Am Dreaming of a White Christmas: The Natural History of a Vision" and "Reading Late at Night, Thermometer Falling," he relies on the frozen moments of memory to explore his emotions concerning his own mortality and the meaning of the past in relation to the discoveries he has achieved during his lifetime. Narrative language gives way to a

---

4. Wordsworth, *Intimations Ode*, in *Selected Poems and Prefaces*, ed. Stillinger, 190.

dreamlike, surreal landscape of symbolic images. In "I Am Dreaming of a White Christmas," Warren envisions his parents sitting in the familiar setting of a family room, but unlike the comforting, spiritual presence he finds in "What Was the Promise?" of *Promises*, the images of his mother and father in this poem are of bodily decay: "Over the shrouded femurs that now are the lap, the hands, / Palm-down, lie" (*CP*, 276). Yet in this dreamscape of physical ruin, a recollected vision of some Christmas long past, the poet notices that "The holly / Is, clearly, fresh" (*CP*, 278), symbolizing not only memory's timelessness but also its persistence.

Juxtaposed against the vision of the past is the *now* of the present—the poet, a grown man standing in Times Square, feeling "Sweat, / Cold in arm-pit" (*CP*, 279) and thinking of "snow falling" in Nez Perce Pass. History, as Warren later writes in *Chief Joseph of the Nez Perce*, may be one collective view of "process," but the microcosm of selfhood is another process that must be explored with equal vigilance:

> All items listed above belong in the world
> In which all things are continuous,
> And are parts of the original dream which
> I am now trying to discover the logic of. This
> Is the process whereby the pain of the past in its pastness
> May be converted into the future tense
> Of joy.
>
> (*CP*, 281)

The last two words of this poem, set apart by literal as well as symbolic space, emphasize the hopefulness of the "oscillating process" of self-discovery—Warren's deepest yearning and intuition that joy, however furtive or elusive, may be realized in the continuity of experience.

The geography of memory, as Warren writes in "Reading Late at Night, Thermometer Falling," is "another country" (*CP*, 315), a place where the unsustainable moment seems to arrest the passage of time. In this poem, Warren revisits a familiar scene from his youth, one that now exists only in his "mind's eye," of his father reading a book. Although the poet does not specify what the title of the book is, he assumes that it is one of his father's countless history books, probably "Hume's *History of England* [or] Roosevelt's *Winning of the West*," or perhaps "Some college text book, or Freud on dreams, abandoned / By one of the children" (*CP*, 311). The exact title is insignificant, for in the poet's memory the book becomes a composite symbol of his father's thirst for knowledge. The poet recollects finding a sheaf of poems his father had written, evidence of the elder Warren's unrealized dreams of accomplishing something beyond his "obligations." Embarrassed by his son's discovery, the father takes the poems from him: "Some kinds of foolishness a man is due to forget, son" (*CP*, 312). This moment, stored in the "Refrigerator of truth," represents for the son the burden of unrealized dreams and the sacrifice of ambitions, rationalized as "foolishness," for the daily "obligations" of life. After his father's death, Warren discovers more of the hidden poems, but to the son, by now an aging man himself and an accomplished poet, the poems are "Not good." But it is not the father's lack of poetic talent that makes an impression upon the son. What is more important, the poet admires the "Indecipherable passion and compulsion" (*CP*, 313) that drove his father to maintain a vision of ideals and truths.

From the vantage point of his maturity, Warren thus achieves what Abrams calls "the central Romantic discovery." It is, Abrams says, that "man is not born for ultimate satisfactions, but in his power to sustain an aspiration that is commensurate with desire, rather than with things as they are, consists man's tragic dignity; and in this recognition of the glory of a hope beyond possibility . . . the mind finds strength and fertilizing joy." Wordsworth finds this joy as he explores his life in *The Prelude*, and Coleridge, despite his extreme bouts of despair and doubt, documents in his late poetry his own discovery of joy and "Hope" that gives "Such strength that he would bless his pains and live."[5] Even Shelley and Keats, who both died before their

---

5. Abrams, *Natural Supernaturalism*, 452–53; Coleridge, "The Visionary Hope," in *Samuel Taylor Coleridge*, ed. Jackson, 131.

thirtieth birthdays, testified to the power of the imagination to heal, reconcile, and ultimately redeem the mind. Throughout *Or Else*, Warren displays his similar faith in the human need to seek truth and to draw on imagination and memory as sources of whatever truths an individual may live by. His father's words in "Reading Late at Night, Thermometer Falling"—"It is terrible for a man to live and not know" (*CP*, 312)—become a legacy for the son, his own truth to pursue and live.

In *Now and Then*, Warren's the desire "just to know" manifests itself not only in the poet's forays into the realm of memory but also in intense, suspended moments of revelation experienced in the world of nature. Justus finds that many of the poems in that volume involve instances in which "individual consciousness seems almost to merge pantheistically with a natural environment . . . as if questions of being might better find answers in such potentially transcendent moments than in the play of logic." In "Rather Like a Dream," perhaps Warren's most direct poetic tribute to Romanticism, the speaker envisions Wordsworth engaging in his own form of truth seeking in nature:

> If Wordsworth, a boy, reached out
> To touch stone or tree to confirm
> His own reality, that wasn't
> So crazy. Or even illogical. For
> We have all done the same, or at least
> Felt the impulse.
>
> (*CP*, 374)

As the poet walks "in the mountain woods, / Alone, hour sunset, season / When the first maple leaf falls red," he feels the same impulse, attempting to "join those moments, and hours, of joy / That dissolve into glitter, like tears" (*CP*, 374) with his present circumstances. With the "summer" of youth long departed and the "drawstring" of mortality drawing "tighter," the speaker pauses to think of the moments of happiness gone "Unrecognized" (*CP*, 375). Echoes of Wordsworth's realization of "The still, sad music of humanity" haunt the speaker:[6] "Old evil and anguish . . . / and the monk-hood / Of darkness grows like a sky over all" (*CP*, 375). Yet the compulsion to know and understand the world compels the speaker, even in the "brooding darkness," to "put out a hand to touch / Tree or stone— just to know" (*CP*, 375). Like his Romantic predecessors, Warren projects a passion to know as well as love the world, and repeatedly in his later poetry, nature serves as the anchor for his abstract considerations of time and identity. Although the self-sufficient unity of nature lies beyond the human grasp, Warren continues his search for the joy that flares "like gasoline spilled / On the cement in a garage . . . / In a blinding blaze, from the filth of the world's floor" (*CP*, 309).

The process of knowledge and self-discovery is never a resolved issue in Warren's work, and in 1979 he returned to *Brother to Dragons* with the hard-earned wisdom and humility he had gained during the intervening twenty-five years. In the new version of his "tale in verse and voices," Warren appears more willing to engage in what Hugh Ruppersburg calls "considerable self-criticism" and "less compelled to attack [Jefferson's] failings" than he had been in the earlier version. We can trace the development of this stance in poems written just prior to the publication of *Brother to Dragons*, especially in "Red-Tail Hawk and Pyre of Youth," another poem from *Now and Then*.[7] The hawk in this poem appears from Warren's earliest verse onward as his

---

6. Justus, *Achievement*, 100; Wordsworth, "Lines Composed a Few Miles above Tintern Abbey," in *Selected Poems and Prefaces*, ed. Stillinger, 110.

7. Ruppersburg, *American Imagination*, 44. Also, Warren dedicated "Red-Tail Hawk and Pyre of Youth" to Harold Bloom, who later edited the *Modern Critical Views* series of essays on Warren's work. Although primarily known as a Romanticist, Bloom followed Warren's career from beginning to end, at times harshly criticizing Warren for his "ideological ferocity" as well as his aversion to Emerson, one of Bloom's acknowledged favorites among American writers. Bloom admits in his essay on the 1979 *Brother to Dragons* that he was "previously cold to Warren's verse" prior to *Incarnations*, but his view of Warren's work changed so radically that he proclaimed Warren's later poetry, especially "Red-Tail Hawk," as some of the best representations of "the American sublime."

most characteristic emblem of imagination and truth, but here the hawk is removed from his natural distance of limitless sky by a young boy and his gun. Warren describes the pure, motiveless joy that accompanies the shooting of the hawk:

> There was no decision in the act,
> There was no choice in the act—the act impossible but
> Possible. I screamed, not knowing
> From what emotion, as at that insane range
> I pressed the cool, snubbed
> Trigger. Saw
> The circle
> Break.
>
> (*CP*, 348)

The boy bears the dead hawk home, "the bloody / Body already to my bare flesh embraced, cuddled / Like babe to heart, and my heart beating like love," and hides it "Like a secret . . . / . . . In the ice chest." In the timeless moment of spotting and shooting the hawk, the boy believes he has attained his own truth, his own communion with the "king of the air" (*CP*, 348). But as Audubon realized in his attempts at merger through art, the boy can only reconstruct a lifeless and imperfect model of his vision, now rendered "Forever earthbound, fit only / For dog tooth, not sky" (*CP*, 349).

With "steel / Driven through to sustain wing and bone," the hawk stands in the poet's boyhood room, regally "perched on its boughcrotch to guard / Blake and *Lycidas*, Augustine, Hardy and *Hamlet*," until the boy becomes a man and leaves his home. In a painful instance of autobiography, Warren relates the losses of adulthood, the years which "pass like a dream, are a dream": ". . . my mother was dead, father bankrupt, and whiskey / Hot in my throat." As his heart throbs "slow in the / Meaningless motion of life," he goes out to the lumber room to find what is left of the stuffed hawk. The hawk is worse for the wear of time, "one eye long gone," like the poet himself, who had suffered the loss of an eye in his youth (". . . and I reckoned / I knew how it felt with one gone") (*CP*, 349). Along with the hawk, the poet finds other relics of his past, an abandoned cache of his once-favored books, the poems he and his friends "had printed in college," and "The collection of sexual Japanese prints—strange sex / Of mechanical sexlessness" (*CP*, 350).

With these items, emblematic of past ambitions and frustrations, the speaker builds a pyre for the hawk:

> Flame flared. Feathers first, and I flinched, then stood
> As the steel wire warped red to defend
> The shape designed godly for air. But
> It fell with the mass, and I
> Did not wait.
>
> (*CP*, 350)

This act, however, does not signal a new beginning for the poet, nor does it purge him of his past. His history is not "thus undone," and if anything, he is forcefully reminded of the realization made in "Original Sin" that "nothing is lost, ever lost" (*CP*, 69). He continues to walk "in the dark, and no stars" (*CP*, 350), his path no clearer than before his attempt to erase the emblems of the past.

Although the physical body of the hawk has been destroyed, its image is preserved in the poet's memory and dreams as a symbolic reminder of that transcendent moment from the past:

> High in the late and uncurdled silver of summer
> The pale vortex appear[s] once again—and you come
> And always the rifle swings up, though with
> The weightlessness now of dream,
> The old .30–30 that knows
> How to bind us in air-blood and earth-blood together
> In our commensurate fate,
> Whose name is a name beyond joy.
>
> (*CP*, 350)

Captured in the stasis of dream and memory, the aim of the rifle becomes the equivalent of the human quest for knowledge and identity, recalling the similar desire for certainty voiced in *Audubon*:

To wake in some dawn and see,
As though down a rifle barrel . . .
The self that is, and there,
Far off but in range, completing that alignment, your fate.

(*CP*, 261)

Such assurance would be "blessedness," but this merging of "air-
blood and earth-blood" is not possible except in the "timelessness" of
memory and imagination. As Warren continually asserts, man must
live in time and "Continue to walk in the world" (*CP*, 261). What
ultimately makes walking in the world bearable, and even joyous, are
those moments when dream and reality intersect. The poet prays that
as death approaches, "While hospital wheel creak beneath / And the
nurse's soles make their *squeak-squeak* like mice," he might again re-
collect the dream of glory "in some last dream or delusion": "And all
will be as it was / In that paradox of unjoyful joyousness" (*CP*, 350).
This vision is not without its price, for he must also remember
"youth's poor, angry, slapdash, and ignorant pyre." Everything in the
dream is the sum total of what the poet has become, the truths he has
achieved, and his share of whatever "blessedness" he has discovered.

Dave Smith describes "Red-Tail Hawk and Pyre of Youth" as a
"mini-Mariner in plot, vision, and construction," Warren's personal
rendering of man's fall and the agonizing journey toward redemption.
In several ways, the poem does parallel Coleridge's fable, but there
are equally significant differences. The act of shooting the hawk is
not what propels the boy into the world of experience and loss—that
much is inevitable—although it does represent a primal scene in
which an ideal of unattainable perfection becomes earthbound, a
"chunk of poor wingless red meat" (*CP*, 349). There is grief and guilt
(the boy hides the hawk, "like a secret"), but there is also "joy past
definition" mingled with "tears past definition" (*CP*, 348). Unlike the
Mariner, who tells his story to the Wedding Guest as a warning
against violating the "sacramental vision of the universe" (*SE*, 266),
the poet/speaker in "Red-Tail Hawk" affirms the necessity, even
compulsion, of transgression. "In separateness only does love learn
definition" (*CP*, 71), Warren says in his early poem "Revelation," and

as he later asserts in "Knowledge and the Image of Man," this love is by nature transgressive: "Man eats of the Tree of Knowledge, and falls. But if he takes another bite, he may get at least a sort of redemption. And a precious redemption" ("Knowledge," 186). In Coleridge's *Rime*, the Mariner's penance is "to teach, by his own example, love and reverence to all things that God made and loveth." Warren, however, insists on the need to take "another bite," to seek not an absolution of the past but to find meaning in it. Bedient contends that Warren, "like Yeats, would be content to live it all again."[8] "Red-Tail Hawk and Pyre of Youth," like Coleridge's poem, recounts the agony of man's fall from innocence, but Warren also offers a vision of the joy that might be salvaged from the wreck of the past.

The 1979 *Brother to Dragons* as well as the last volumes of poetry reveal Warren's long process of self-examination and the realizations he achieved in maturity. Rather than excoriating Jefferson from the lofty vantage point of hindsight, Warren joins his quest for identity with that of the former president. Margaret Mills Harper has observed in her examination of the two versions of *Brother to Dragons*, that "R.P.W. in the 1979 version more clearly parallels, rather than leads, Jefferson in his search for knowledge."[9] The stance Warren assumes in the later version is one of personal humility, an acceptance of his position as a man looking up rather than one looking down on the world in disgust. We see Warren in "Heart of Autumn" with his "face lifted now skyward" (*CP*, 377), watching geese fly south for the winter. These geese, like the ones in the last section of *Audubon* that the poet recalls from his boyhood, symbolize the unity of nature that the poet longs for but cannot achieve ("I did not know what was happening in my heart") (*CP*, 266). Some will suffer the same fate as the

8. Dave Smith, "He Prayeth Best Who Lovest Best," *American Poetry Review* 8 (January–February 1979): 6; Coleridge, *The Rime of the Ancient Mariner*, in *Samuel Taylor Coleridge*, ed. Jackson, 65; Bedient, *In the Heart's Last Kingdom*, 186.

9. Margaret Mills Harper, "Versions of History and *Brother to Dragons*," in *Robert Penn Warren's* Brother to Dragons: *A Discussion*, ed. James A. Grimshaw, Jr. (Baton Rouge: Louisiana State University Press, 1983), 237.

hawk in "Red-Tail Hawk and Pyre of Youth," the *boom*, the lead pellet" of a hunter's gun, but others will "stagger, recover control, / Then take the last glide for a far glint of water" (*CP*, 376).

Like the hawk that appears throughout Warren's poetry, the geese are unaware of their "destiny," whether it be reaching the end of their journey or falling prey to the hunter ("None / Knows what has happened"). Watching the geese instinctively and "Tirelessly" follow the "season's logic," the human observer wonders, "Do I know my own story?" At least the geese "know / When the hour comes for the great wing-beat . . . The path of pathlessness, with all the joy / Of destiny fulfilling its own name." Conscious of both mortality and the inchoate longing for purpose and identity, the speaker reflects on the pathlessness of human life: "I have known time and distance, but not why I am here" (*CP*, 376). The geese have no reason to "know" themselves; they *are* themselves. Like Keats's nightingale, they partake of their own immortality by the yearning that they invoke.

The wistful tone of "Heart of Autumn" does not mean that Warren desires a life of instinct rather than of mental action, however painful consciousness may be. We are not like the sheep he describes in "A Way to Love God" whose "stupid" eyes "Stared into nothingness" (*CP*, 325), nor are we as fortunate as the bear in *Audubon* who "feels his own fat / Sweeten, like a drowse, deep to the bone" (*CP*, 254). Instead, the geese become the symbol of human aspiration. They exist in a fullness of being that the poet finds ideal, and although he cannot merge with nature, he can at least identify with the sublimity the geese represent:

> Hearing the high beat, my arms outstretched in the tingling
> Process of transformation, and soon tough legs,
> With folded feet, trail in the sounding vacuum of passage.
>
> (*CP*, 377)

While the body may be trapped in time, the imagination can transport the mind into realms of supernal oneness. In this "spot of time," the poet's heart "is impacted with a fierce impulse / To unwordable utterance—Toward sunset, at a great height." For Warren, as for the

Romantics, such transcendent vision does not translate into the desire to leave the natural world behind in favor of other worlds. Whatever transcendence that is to be gained must be rooted in the physical world. Yet, despite life's "pathlessness"—"Path of logic, path of folly all / The same" (*CP*, 377)—joy and strength are the ultimate rewards of the search for knowledge.

In his later poetry, Warren acknowledges that it "takes a long time" to achieve "Heart-hope, undefinable, verging to tears / Of happiness and the soul's calm" (*CP*, 537). The "oscillating process" (*DP*, 93) that governs the search for identity has its heights, but these heights must be earned by the harrowing of private valleys. Alienation, despair, and even annihilation threaten those in Warren's poetry and fiction who descend into the valleys of human experience. The heights, however, offer the promise of joy and renewed possibilities, made all the more glorious by the peace achieved in the process. The themes that Warren found central in Coleridge—"the broken tabu, the torments of guilt and punishment, the joy of reconciliation" (*SE*, 271)—appear throughout his own work from beginning to end, but in his later work "the joy of reconciliation" emerges with greater frequency. Often in the poems of his last two decades we encounter Warren's most ecstatic moments of transcendence, especially in *Altitudes and Extensions*, his last collection of poetry.[10] In "Delusion?— No!" the poet stands on a mountaintop (a setting that occurs often in his later poems) and gazes at the sky above him and the earth below:

> In that divine osmosis I stood
> And felt each discrete and distinct stroke
> Of the heart as it downward fled—
> Cliff, cleft, gorge, chasm, and, far off,
> Ravine cut in the flattening but still high glitter
> Of earth.
> . . . I entered in.

10. The poems from *Altitudes and Extensions* will be cited as they appear in *CP*.

Was part of all. I knew the
Glorious light of inner darkness burn
Like the fundamental discovery.

(*CP*, 581)

This moment of "divine osmosis" sounds suspiciously Emersonian,
reinforcing Harold Bloom's argument that Warren's later poetry is
"uneasily indebted to Emerson."[11] Yet the uneasiness is conspicuously
evident. Unlike Emerson's moments of transcendence, Warren's
fleeting experiences of "divine osmosis" take him earthward, not skyward.

Warren expressed a lifelong distaste for Emerson's transcenden-
talism, and in an earlier poem, "Homage to Emerson, on Night
Flight to New York" (1966), the poet sarcastically states that "At
38,000 feet Emerson / Is dead right" (*CP*, 194). Although Emerson
appropriated much of his philosophy from the English Romantics
(Coleridge in particular), in his early works he does not acknowledge
the fallen world that the Romantics perceived, nor does he allow for
the limitations of human insight. Only later in life does Emerson
offer a more chastened vision of humanity: "It is very unhappy but
too late to be helped, the discovery we have made that we exist. That
discovery is called the Fall of Man. Ever afterwards we suspect our
instruments."[12] From the beginning of his career, Warren's vision of
humanity includes an awareness of the sad knowledge that Emerson
belatedly achieved. Yet, in his later poetry, Warren increasingly insists
on the human need for transcendence, even if it is circumscribed by

11. Bloom, "Sunset Hawk," in *Modern Critical Views*, ed. Bloom, 199.

12. Warren told Marshall Walker in a 1969 interview that "Emerson can-
cels evil out of the human algebra. . . . I really have something that's almost
a pathological flinch from Emersonianism . . . from these oversimplifications,
as I think of them, of the grinding problems of life and of personality" (Warren, "An Interview," in *Talking with Robert Penn Warren*, ed. Watkins et al.,
153, 155. The excerpt from Emerson is taken from "Experience," in *Selections
from Ralph Waldo Emerson*, ed. Stephen E. Whicher (Boston: Houghton
Mifflin, 1957), 269.

the limitations of existence. One might say that Warren, after a lifetime of searching for meaning, made a tentative peace with Emerson. Significantly, Warren's last novel, *A Place to Come To*, offers the most fully realized Romantic vision of reconciliation and acceptance in his fiction. Jediah Tewksbury, a modern wanderer who must discover purpose and meaning out of his own "pathlessness" (*CP*, 376), attempts to escape his poor-white background and the legends of his late father's infamous sexual prowess by fleeing his hometown in Alabama. In a form of spiritual autobiography similar to Jack Burden's story, *A Place to Come To* relates Jed's first-person account of his journey toward self-knowledge and his final realization that flight, whether physical, psychological, sexual, or philosophical, is ultimately futile.

Despite his attempts at evasion, Jed belatedly discovers that "nothing is lost, ever lost" (*CP*, 69). Even in his sexual encounters with Rozelle Hardcastle (a fellow fugitive from Dugton, Alabama, both geographically and spiritually), he realizes that their love-making is only "the clutch, struggle, and spasm" of "barren simplicity": "As for the love-making, it was becoming a rather marginal feature of the assignations, obsessive but marginal and—to adapt Thomas Hobbes's description of life—nasty, brutish, and short. It was both an interruption of, and a flight from, the scarcely specified struggle between us" (*PCT*, 231). In his smug unawareness, Jed asserts that selfhood "is the moment of perception between pastlessness and futurelessness," but this "revelation" (*PCT*, 235), like Jack Burden's theory of the Great Twitch, overlooks the past that must, as in all of Warren's works, be acknowledged and accepted.

After all the "intensities, lies, self-divisions, dubieties, duplicities, and blind and variously devised plummetings into timeless sexuality" that characterize his life, Jed marries his college lover, Dauphine Finkel, then fathers a son, divorces, and settles into the "routines and nags" of middle-aged life. Despite the spiritual battering that he has taken, there is a final reconciliation to be achieved. After the death of his mother, who had encouraged him with protective fierceness to "get shet" of Dugton, Jed returns home. As he gazes on the seemingly insignificant tokens of his childhood, he feels each object "glow with

a special assertion of its being—of my being, too, as though only
now, after all the years, I was returning to my final self, long lost"
(*PCT*, 332). Justus points out that "this retrospective visit . . . does
more than bring an 'elegiac dampness' to his eye; returning to his lost
self means also the birth, belated as it is, of concern and responsibility
for needs that are less grand or petty than they are merely human."[13]
What Jed has achieved is a vision of the past as something vital and
significant, not only for the present but for the future as well. His
"place to come to" emerges as the literal place of his birth, but this
patria is also the unmapped region of "that landscape lost in the
heart's homely deep" (*CP*, 131), as Warren writes in "Lullaby: Moonlight Lingers." "We are all stuck with trying to find the meaning of
our lives," Jed states in his newfound wisdom, "and the only thing we
have to work on, or with, is our past" (*PCT*, 145). At the end of the
novel, Jed at last realizes "the blessedness of knowing that men were
real, and brothers in their reality," and he envisions a benedictory
gesture toward his son: "I could point out to him all the spots that I
had dreamed of pointing out to him" (*PCT*, 341). Like the blessing
Warren extends to his son Gabriel in *Promises*, Jed's awareness of
life's possibilities deepens his sense of continuity, of "looking with joy
upon the irremediable things."[14]

A Place to Come To is not Warren's best novel, and in many ways
it lacks the tragic depth of such earlier novels as *All the King's Men*
and *World Enough and Time*. Some readers may find Jed's journey
toward redemption too programmatic and sentimental. Yet it does
affirm the same Romantic ideals that find more eloquent expression
in Warren's poetry. Following in the tradition of the Romantics,
Wordsworth and Yeats in particular, Warren uses memory combined
with the discoveries achieved in maturity to provide insight toward
the relationship between the self and what John Crowe Ransom
called "the world's body."[15] In its final phase, Warren's Romanticism

13. Justus, *Achievement*, 316.

14. Warren, "A Conversation with Cleanth Brooks," in *The Possibilities
of Order*, ed. Simpson, 26.

15. John Crowe Ransom, *The World's Body* (Baton Rouge: Louisiana
State University Press, 1968), 5.

more closely resembles that of Yeats than any of the early Romantics.
Only Wordsworth and Coleridge lived into what might be considered old age, and as Hilton Kramer, Harold Bloom, and George
Bornstein have noted, late in these poets' lives the power that had
generated their earlier works had diminished considerably.

Such was not Warren's fate. Even in his seventies, he projected
into his work the passion of a man driven to explore "Life's truth." In
"American Portrait: Old Style," the poet lies down in a ditch he and
his childhood friend K. once played in and ponders "What it would
be like to die, . . . / And know yourself dead lying under / the infinite
motion of the sky" (*CP*, 342). Yet this contemplation is only temporary:

> But why should I lie here longer?
> I am not dead yet, though in years,
> And the world's way is yet long to go,
> And I love the world even in my anger,
> And love is a hard thing to outgrow.
>
> (*CP*, 342)

Like Yeats, Warren insists that the ability to "love the world" depends
on a continuing sense of loss, even experiencing it anew. Reflecting
on his long poetic career, Yeats wrote in *Mythologies* that "a poet,
when he is growing old, will ask himself if he cannot keep his mask
and his vision without new bitterness, new disappointment. . . . Then
he will remember Wordsworth withering into eighty years, honoured
and empty-witted, and climb to some waste room and find, forgotten
there by youth, some bitter crust."[16] Warren chose not to "wither." In
"Mortal Limit," one of his final published poems, we again see his
hawk ascend into the "dream-spectral light" of triumphant vision:

> . . . Beyond what height
> Hangs now the black speck? Beyond what range will gold eyes see

16. Wiliam Butler Yeats, *Mythologies* (London: Macmillan, 1962), 342.

New ranges rise to mark the last scrawl of light?
Or, having tasted that atmosphere's thinness, does it
Hang motionless in dying vision before
It knows it will accept the mortal limit,
And swing into the great circular downwardness that will restore
The breath of earth? Of rock? Of rot? Of other such
Items, and the darkness of whatever dream we clutch?

(*CP*, 531)

This dream of the unattainable, of striving beyond the "mortal limit," is the signature impulse of Warren's Romantic vision. Yet even in the last, most visionary of his poems, we note the absence of substantive resolutions; "Mortal Limit" ends with questions unanswered despite the intensity of the poet's expressed need to understand what the world *means*. It is this struggle to read the signs and semiotics of nature and experience that gives Warren's later verse its power. "The whole world pours at us," one voice in *Now and Then* declares. "But the code book, somehow, is lost" (*CP*, 360). Throughout his work, Warren conveys the sense that the answers to his ontological and epistemological questions will never be fully realized. The questioning, in itself, offers a source of significance.

Above all, Warren's Romantic vision emphasizes fully realized humanity, and like his Romantic precursors, he insists that the imagination must find its materials in basic human experience. The development of Warren's Romanticism throughout his career does not suggest a movement from the irresolute longings of youth to the confirmed wisdom of maturity. Instead, his mature poetry reveals his increasing awareness of the agonizing relativity of truth. What emerges as one of the most significant discoveries explored in his poetry from the 1940s onward is the possibility of joy and hope, what Wordsworth called the "Strength in what remains behind"[17] His early poetry, more influenced by Eliot, depicts a world similar to Jack Burden's: "The

17. Wordsworth, *Intimations Ode*, in *Selected Poems and Prefaces*, ed. Stillinger, 190.

world then was simply an accumulation of items, odds and ends of things like the broken and misused and dust-shrouded things gathered in a garret" (*AKM*, 189). From *Promises* to the end of his career, Warren's assertion of the individual's "continual and intimate interpenetration" ("Knowledge," 185) with the rest of humanity takes on strength and purpose, offering a vision of the "joy in which all joys should rejoice" (*CP*, 108). With his emphasis on the "osmosis of being" ("Knowledge," 185) that binds humanity and his belief in the sustaining power of the imagination, Warren takes his place in the Romantic tradition as an ardent truth seeker whose vision encompasses both the tragedy and the passion of life.

Bibliography

Works by Robert Penn Warren

"A Conversation with Cleanth Brooks." In *The Possibilities of Order: Cleanth Brooks and His Work,* edited by Lewis P. Simpson. Baton Rouge: Louisiana State University Press, 1976.

All the King's Men. New York: Harcourt Brace Jovanovich, 1946.

Brother to Dragons: A Tale in Verse and Voices. New York: Random House, 1953.

Brother to Dragons: A Tale in Verse and Voices, A New Version. New York: Random House, 1979.

The Collected Poems of Robert Penn Warren, edited by John Burt. Baton Rouge: Louisiana State University Press, 1998.

Democracy and Poetry. Cambridge: Harvard University Press, 1975.

"Knowledge and the Image of Man." *Sewanee Review* 63 (spring 1955): 182–92.

"Love and Knowledge in Eudora Welty." In *Selected Essays.* New York: Random House, 1951.

New and Selected Essays. New York: Random House, 1989.

Night Rider. New York: Random House, 1939.

A Place to Come To. New York: Random House, 1977.

Portrait of a Father. Lexington: University Press of Kentucky, 1988.

"The Present State of Poetry: III. In the United States." *Kenyon Review* 1 (autumn 1939): 384–98.

"Pure and Impure Poetry." In *Selected Essays*. New York: Random House, 1958).

Selected Essays. New York: Random House, 1951.

World Enough and Time: A Romantic Novel. New York: Random House, 1950.

Other Works

Abrams, M. H. *The Mirror and the Lamp: Romantic Theory and the Critical Tradition*. New York: Norton, 1953.

———. *Natural Supernaturalism: Tradition and Revolution in Romantic Literature*. New York: Norton, 1971.

Barthes, Roland. "The Rhetoric of the Image." In *Classic Essays on Photography*, edited by Alan Trachtenberg. New Haven, Conn.: Leete's Island Books, 1980.

Bedient, Calvin. *In the Heart's Last Kingdom: Robert Penn Warren's Major Poetry*. Cambridge: Harvard University Press, 1984.

Bergonzi, Bernard. *T. S. Eliot*. New York: Macmillan, 1972.

Berman, Art. *From the New Criticism to Deconstruction: The Reception of Structuralism and Poststructuralism*. Urbana: University of Illinois Press, 1988.

Bloom, Harold. Review of *Brother to Dragons*, by Robert Penn Warren. *New Republic*, September 30, 1978, p. 34.

———. *The Visionary Company: A Reading of English Romantic Poetry*. Ithaca: Cornell University Press, 1971.

———, ed. *Modern Critical Views: Robert Penn Warren*. New York: Chelsea House, 1986.

Blotner, Joseph. *Robert Penn Warren: A Biography*. New York: Random House, 1997.

———. "Romantic Elements in Faulkner." In *Romantic and Modern: Revaluations of Literary Tradition*, edited by George Bornstein. Pittsburgh: University of Pittsburgh Press, 1977.

Blum, Morgan. "*Promises* as Fulfillment." *Kenyon Review* 21 (winter 1959): 97–120.

Bohner, Charles H. *Robert Penn Warren*. New York: Twayne, 1964.

Bornstein, George. *Transformations of Romanticism in Yeats, Eliot, and Stevens*. Chicago: University of Chicago Press, 1976.

Brooks, Cleanth. "Afterword." *Southern Quarterly* 31 (summer 1993): 106–12.

————. *The Hidden God: Studies in Hemingway, Faulkner, Yeats, Eliot, and Warren.* New Haven: Yale University Press, 1963.

Brown, Homer Obed. "The Art of Theology and the Theology of Art: Robert Penn Warren's Reading of Coleridge's *The Rime of the Ancient Mariner.*" *Boundary: A Journal of Postmodern Literature and Culture* 8 (fall 1979): 237–60.

Burneko, Grace Bailey. "Innocence Recaptured: In 'Composition in Gold and Red-Gold.'" *Southern Quarterly* 31 (summer 1993): 95–100.

Casper, Leonard. *Robert Penn Warren: The Dark and Bloody Ground.* Seattle: University of Washington Press, 1960.

Clark, William Bedford. "Young Warren and the Problematics of Faith." *Mississippi Quarterly* 45 (winter 1991–92): 29–39.

Cluck, Nancy. "Audubon: Images of the Artist in Eudora Welty and Robert Penn Warren." *Southern Literary Journal* 17 (spring 1985): 41–53.

Coleridge, Samuel Taylor. *A Critical Edition of the Major Works*, edited by H. J. Jackson. Oxford: Oxford University Press, 1985.

Cowan, Louise. *The Fugitive Group: A Literary History.* Baton Rouge: Louisiana State University Press, 1959.

Cowley, Malcolm, ed. *Writers at Work.* New York: Random House, 1959.

Dickey, James. "In the Presence of Anthologies." *Sewanee Review* 66 (spring 1958): 308.

Donne, John. "The Canonization." In *Seventeenth-Century Poetry and Prose*, edited by Alexander M. Witherspoon and Frank J. Warnke. New York: Harcourt Brace Jovanovich, 1982.

Dupee, F. W. "RPW and Others." *Nation* 25 (October 1944): 660, 662.

Eliot, T. S. "Baudelaire." In *Selected Essays.* New York: Harcourt, Brace and World, 1964.

————. *Collected Poems, 1909–1962.* New York: Harcourt Brace Jovanovich, 1963.

————. *The Use of Poetry and the Use of Criticism: Studies in the Relation of Criticism to Poetry in England.* Cambridge: Harvard University Press, 1961.

————. Emerson, Ralph Waldo. "Experience." In *Selections from Ralph Waldo Emerson*, edited by Stephen E. Whicher. Boston: Houghton Mifflin, 1957.

Ferris, William. "Robert Penn Warren: 'My Cup Ran Over.'" *Reckon: The Magazine of Southern Culture* 1 (Premiere issue, 1995): 125–27.

Fitts, Dudley. "Of Tragic Stature." *Poetry* 65 (November 1944): 94–101.

Friar, Kimon, and John Malcolm Brinnin, eds., *Modern Poetry: British and American.* New York: Appleton-Century-Crofts, 1951.

Frost, Robert. "The Oven Bird." In *Complete Poems of Robert Frost.* New York: Holt, Rinehart and Winston, 1964.

Graziano, Frank, ed. *Homage to Robert Penn Warren: A Collection of Critical Essays.* Durango, Colo.: Logbridge-Rhodes, 1981.

Gregory, Horace. "Of Vitality, Regionalism, and Satire in Recent American Poetry." *Sewanee Review* 52 (autumn 1944): 572–93.

Harper, Margaret Mills. "Versions of History and *Brother to Dragons.*" In *Robert Penn Warren's* Brother to Dragons: *A Discussion,* edited by James A. Grimshaw, Jr. Baton Rouge: Louisiana State University Press, 1983.

Hendricks, Randy J. "Warren's Wandering Son." *South Atlantic Review* 59 (May 1994): 75–93.

Hummer, T. R. "Robert Penn Warren: Audubon and the Moral Center." *Southern Review* 16 (autumn 1980): 803–10.

Jack, Peter Munro. Review of *Eleven Poems on the Same Theme,* by Robert Penn Warren. *New York Times Book Review* 26 (April 1942): 4.

Jancovich, Mark. *The Cultural Politics of the New Criticism.* Cambridge: Cambridge University Press, 1933.

Justus, James H. *The Achievement of Robert Penn Warren.* Baton Rouge: Louisiana State University Press, 1981.

Keats, John. *Selected Poems.* Edited by John Barnard. New York: Penguin, 1988.

Kenner, Hugh. "Bradley." In *T. S. Eliot: A Collection of Critical Essays,* edited by Hugh Kenner. Englewood Cliffs, N.J.: Prentice-Hall, 1962.

Kermode, Frank. *Romantic Image.* London: Routledge and Kegan Paul, 1957.
———. *The Sense of an Ending.* London: Routledge and Kegan Paul, 1967.

Kramer, Hilton. "Robert Penn Warren and His Poetry: An Introduction." In *Homage to Robert Penn Warren: A Collection of Critical Essays.* Durango, Colo.: Logbridge-Rhodes, 1981.

Kroeber, Karl. *Romantic Narrative Art.* Madison: University of Wisconsin Press, 1960.

Mariani, Paul. "Robert Penn Warren." In *Modern Critical Views: Robert Penn Warren,* edited by Harold Bloom. New York: Chelsea House, 1986.

Marrs, Suzanne. "John James Audubon in Fiction and Poetry: Literary Portraits by Eudora Welty and Robert Penn Warren." *Southern Studies: An Interdisciplinary Journal of the South* 20 (winter 1981): 378–83.

Martz, Louis L. "Recent Poetry; Established Idiom." *Yale Review* 59 (1970): 566.

——. "The Virtues of Collection." *Yale Review* 50 (spring 1961): 445–46.

Matthiessen, F. O. "American Poetry Now." *Kenyon Review* 6 (autumn 1944): 683–96.

——. *American Renaissance: Art and Expression in the Age of Emerson and Whitman*. Oxford: Oxford University Press, 1941.

McDowell, Frederick P. W. "Psychology and Theme in *Brother to Dragons*." *PMLA* 70 (September 1955): 572.

Mill, John Stuart. *Autobiography*. London: Oxford University Press, 1924.

Milton, John. *Paradise Lost*. In *Complete Poems and Major Prose*, edited by Merritt Y. Hughes. New York: Macmillan, 1957.

Pratt, William. *The Fugitive Poets: Modern Southern Poetry in Perspective*. Nashville: J. S. Sanders, 1991.

Rahv, Philip. "Paleface and Redskin." *Sewanee Review* (Premiere issue, 1939): 251–56.

Raiziss, Sona. *The Metaphysical Passion: Seven Modern American Poets and the Seventeenth-Century Tradition*. Philadelphia: University of Pennsylvania Press, 1952.

Ransom, John Crowe. "The Inklings of 'Original Sin.' " *Saturday Review* 20 (May 1944): 10–11.

——. *The World's Body*. Baton Rouge: Louisiana State University Press, 1968.

Runyon, Randolph Paul. "Repeating the 'Implacable Monotone' in *Thirty-Six Poems*." *Mississippi Quarterly* 48 (winter 1994–95): 39–56.

Ruppersburg, Hugh. *Robert Penn Warren and the American Imagination*. Athens: University of Georgia Press, 1990.

Sczcesiul, Anthony. "Robert Penn Warren's *Audubon*: Vision and Revision." *Mississippi Quarterly* 47 (winter 1993–94): 3–14.

Shelley, Percy Bysshe. *Shelley's Poetry and Prose*, edited by Donald H. Reiman and Sharon B. Powers. New York: Norton, 1977.

Shepherd, Allen. "Warren's Audubon: 'Issue in Purer Form' and 'The Ground Rules of Fact.' " *Mississippi Quarterly* 24 (winter 1970): 47–56.

Smith, Dave. "He Prayeth Best Who Loveth Best." *American Poetry Review* 8 (January–February 1979): 4–8.

Southard, W. P. "Speculation I: The Religious Poetry of Robert Penn Warren." *Kenyon Review* 7 (autumn 1945): 653–76.

Stewart, John L. *The Burden of Time: The Fugitives and Agrarians*. Princeton, N.J.: Princeton University Press, 1965.

Strandberg, Victor. *A Colder Fire: The Poetry of Robert Penn Warren*. Westport, Conn.: Greenwood Press, 1965.

———. "Image and Persona in Warren's 'Early' Poetry." *Mississippi Quarterly* 37 (spring 1984): 135–48.

———. *The Poetic Vision of Robert Penn Warren.* Lexington: University Press of Kentucky, 1977.

Tate, Allen. "To a Romantic." In *Collected Poems, 1919–1976.* New York: Farrar Straus Giroux, 1977.

Untermeyer, Louis. "Cream of the Verse." Review of *Eleven Poems on the Same Theme,* by Robert Penn Warren. *Yale Review* 32 (winter 1943): 366.

Waggoner, Hyatt H. *American Poets: From the Puritans to the Present.* Boston: Houghton Mifflin, 1968.

Walker, Marshall. *Robert Penn Warren: A Vision Earned.* New York: Harper and Row, 1979.

Wallace, Patricia. "Warren, with Ransom and Tate." In *The Columbia History of American Poetry,* edited by Jay Parini. New York: Columbia University Press, 1993.

Watkins, Floyd C. "To Emerson with Love: A Rattlesnake from Robert Penn Warren." *Mississippi Quarterly* 36 (spring 1983): 91–103.

Watkins, Floyd C., John T. Hiers, and Mary Louise Weaks, eds. *Talking with Robert Penn Warren.* Athens: University of Georgia Press, 1990.

Webb, Max. "*Audubon: A Vision*: Robert Penn Warren's Response to Eudora Welty's 'A Still Moment.'" *Mississippi Quarterly* 34 (fall 1981): 445–55.

Wordsworth, William. *Selected Poems and Prefaces,* edited by Jack Stillinger. Boston: Houghton Mifflin, 1965.

———. *The Prelude.* Edited by Jonathan Wordsworth, M. H. Abrams, and Stephen Gill. New York: Norton, 1979.

Yeats, William Butler. *Mythologies.* London: Macmillan, 1962.

———. *Selected Poems and Three Plays,* edited by M. L. Rosenthal. New York: Collier Books, 1986.

Index